W9-DCZ-497

Airbrush Illustration for Architecture

George Dombek
and Tom Porter

Airbrush Illustration for Architecture

Illustrations by Sue Goodman

W. W. Norton & Company
New York • London

Dedicated to the memory of Jim Stanley Dombek

Page 1: *Jail Number 6,* 40 x 60 in (102 x 152 cm), by George Dombek
Pages 2–3: *San Francisco Fire Escape,* 30 x 42 in (76 x 107 cm),
by George Dombek

Printed in Singapore
First Edition

Manufacturing by KHL
Book design by Gilda Hannah
Production manager: Leeann Graham

Library of Congress Cataloging-in-Publication Data

Dombek, George.
Airbrush illustration for architecture / George Dombek and Tom Porter; illustrations by Sue Goodman.
p. cm.
Includes index.
ISBN 0-393-73022-0
1. Architectural drawing-Technique. 2. Airbrush art. I. Porter, Tom. II. Goodman, Sue. III. Title.

NA2726.D66 2003
743 .84-dc21 2003042194

W. W. Norton & Company, Inc., 500 Fifth Avenue,
New York, N.Y. 10110
www.wwnorton.com

W. W. Norton & Company Ltd., Castle House, 75/76 Wells St.,
London W1T 3QT

0 9 8 7 6 5 4 3 2 1

Contents

Acknowledgments

We would like to thank Dean Rodner B. Wright for his generous support and the following students of George Dombek's airbrush workshops for making their impressive work available for publication: Tony Benton, Thaddeus Bryniarski, Jorge Calderon, Augustus Cooper, Coy Cornelius, Roland Costellanos, Ken Cureton, Joseph Dougherty, James Dulock, Peter Gonzalez, Rob Hall, Bret Hammond, Rhonda Hammond, Orlando Harris, Jose Jaramillo, Ernesto Lluesma, Jon Mathras, Crystal McIntosh, Stewart Nelson, Adam Pelsky, Karen Pennycooke, Trent Price, Greg Register, Igor Reyes, Phillip Rittner, Arnold Rivera, James Rose, Francisco Simmons, John Tice, Keith White, and Scott Wolff.

We also thank the manufacturers who supplied additional technical information, materials, and examples of their products for testing. These include Arches Papers, Badger Airbrush Co., Golden Artist Colors, Inc., H. K. Holbein, Medea Airbrush Products, Paasche Airbrush Company, and Winsor & Newton.

Very special thanks are due to Kirk Lybecker, technical consultant to Medea Arttool, for his unstinting support, enthusiasm, and technical assistance in the production of chapter 2.

Finally, we would like to extend deep appreciation to our editor, Nancy Green, who, displaying the patience of a saint, has shepherded this project from inception to fruition.

Introduction

The airbrush has a remarkable genealogy. Thousands of years ago the ancient precursor of today's precision-engineered airbrush was a hollow bone through which prehistoric man blew color from his pigment-loaded mouth. Evidence of this practice is seen in the sprayed outlines of hands found alongside cave paintings such as those at El Castillo in Santander, Spain, where prehistoric artists placed one splayed hand on the cave wall and used it as a "mask" to create an "airbrushed" silhouette. But why, in our instant-gratification, digital age, should we architectural designers contemplate taking up the airbrush? There are several reasons. First, the airbrush has a remarkable ability to record the behavior of light as it falls across the surfaces of plane and form. No other medium can so effortlessly and convincingly depict this allusive phenomenon. Moreover, as the nature of the marks made by this medium come so close to the way that we perceive architectural form, its rendering ability directly harnesses a medium to the very manner in which we perceive, visualize, and comprehend architecture.

Additionally, as we have become more reliant on the computer as a design tool, we have begun to lose touch with the art of drawing. According to Alan Davidson, head of the computer graphics firm Hayes Davidson, many of today's architectural graduates have little or no drawing ability. Although they can generate instant and impressive electronic images, they have little understanding of how a compelling image works. This, he concludes, is due to a lack of experience in direct observational drawing. In other words, we have stopped seeing.

Decrying the fact that children can be introduced to the computer from as early as 13 months, "False Promise," a cover story in *Newsweek* (September 25, 2000), underscores this observation. One study cited the fact that although children exposed to developmental software showed significant gains in intelligence, nonverbal skills, and long-term memory, their dimension of creativity had fallen by up to 50 percent. The virtual world, it seems, begins to overshadow the real world and erode the inspirational richness of our multisensory experience of it. These findings are echoed in the writings of Jean Baudrillard, who suggests that the reality of the modern world is becoming indistinguishable from a simulated version in which a fake hyperreality is enjoyed for its own sake—a confusion exploited in myriad movie storylines.

A more recent development has been the Campaign for Drawing, a foundation dedicated to encouraging the reinstatement of freehand drawing in architectural education. With several signature architects among its membership, the group aims to redress the balance between digital and freehand mark-making, citing the act of directly drawing and visualizing on paper as being fundamental to innovation and originality in the architectural design process. As if to underscore Louis Sullivan's plea for a "ten-fingered grasp on reality," the value of drawing is also endorsed by Richard Meier, who, writing in the March 2002 edition of *Architectural Digest*, advises architectural students ". . . not to ignore their drawing skills. While the computer has brought a lot of advantages, it can never replace the ability to draw well." Indeed, while computer software can simulate the freehand mediums of drawing, sketching, painting, and airbrushing, its electronic wizardry in imitating and creating superficially dazzling images not only erects an obstacle between our perception and the stimulus of the real world, but also disguises a multitude of inadequacies in our pictorial abilities.

Connecting the eye and brain to the hand is an exhilarating experience and is critical to the production of high-quality architectural images. This book introduces the airbrush as an extension of our perception and as a direct means of creating considered, credible, compelling images.

1 Gallery: Student Illustrations

To illustrate the enormous potential of the airbrush, we have selected a group of airbrush work by students from Florida A & M University's School of Architecture. These illustrations were completed as part of George Dombek's airbrush workshop, an introductory elective course for beginners. We hope that these illustrations, produced by relative novices, will inspire you to embark on the exercises outlined in this book and ultimately indulge in the sharply focused world of the airbrush medium.

Each illustration is based on preliminary photographic assignments or design magazine searches in which the central aim was to find and develop a source image powerful enough to engage the attention of the viewer. Although airbrush illustrations can be produced from observational drawing (and some of the book's exercises encourage this), we see no problem with using the voracious eye of the camera as a starting point for an airbrush illustration. This is because its clarity and precision are highly sympathetic to the photorealistic potential of the spray medium.

The selection of the source image is

1.1 Façade, 8 x 12 in (20 x 30 cm)

crucial—each original, be it slide, print, or drawing, must be critically assessed in terms of pictorial content, composition, and, of course, visual impact (see pages 94–95). Once the source image has been approved, it is subjected to recropping to maximize its compositional impact. The next stage involves the careful preplanning of the airbrushing sequence, including drawing the artwork, cutting the mask, and working out the spraying sequence. This stage is also crucial to the ultimate success of the illustration. However, although the entire production process should be thoroughly preplanned, there is always room for experimentation and happy accidents. All illustrations in the gallery, except where indicated, are 18 x 21 in (46 x 53 cm) produced on a 22 x 30 in (56 x 76 cm) Crescent illustration board. For short descriptions of the techniques used to achieve these illustrations, see appendix A.

1.2 Villa Savoye, Poissy

1.3 Architectural detail

1.4 Architectural detail

1.5 Industrial plant

1.6 Entrance

1.7 Frank O. Gehry's The Experience Music Project, Seattle

1.8 Atrium, Miami

1.9 Grid portal

1.10 Cornice

1.11 Frieze detail

1.12 Materials montage

1.13 Kahn Residence, Pacific Palisades, California

1.14 Richard Meier's Smith House, Darien, Connecticut

1.15 Kimbell Art Museum, Fort Worth, Texas

1.16 Light transitions

1.17 Study model

1.18 Interior

1.19 Elevation detail

1.20 Science Museum at the City of Arts and Sciences, Valencia

2 Airbrush Equipment and Basic Operation

The airbrush is a highly engineered precision instrument, so, to get the most out of it, you must first understand how it works. An airbrush alone is not enough to create an illustration; you also need an air supply to propel the medium. This section recommends the most appropriate equipment, paints, and illustration surfaces.

AIRBRUSHES

There are more than a dozen airbrush manufacturers, some of them producing as many as twenty different models. With such a wide selection in the art stores it is wise to evaluate their performance in relation to their cost. Different airbrush models are designed to serve different spraying functions. They fall into the following categories.

External-Mix Airbrushes

As their name implies, external-mix airbrushes (fig. 2.1) use paint that is diffused with air outside of and away from the head of the airbrush. Consequently, the jet of air has little opportunity to thoroughly mix with the paint, resulting in an atomized dot pattern on the painted surface. Essentially, external-mix airbrushes work like small spray guns with the paint being fed from a reservoir mounted underneath the handset. They have a setting for paint volume that is separate from the airflow trigger, which means that the volume of pigment flow must be preset. This makes changing the volume of paint during spraying an awkward endeavor for all but the most skilled operator. For this reason, this

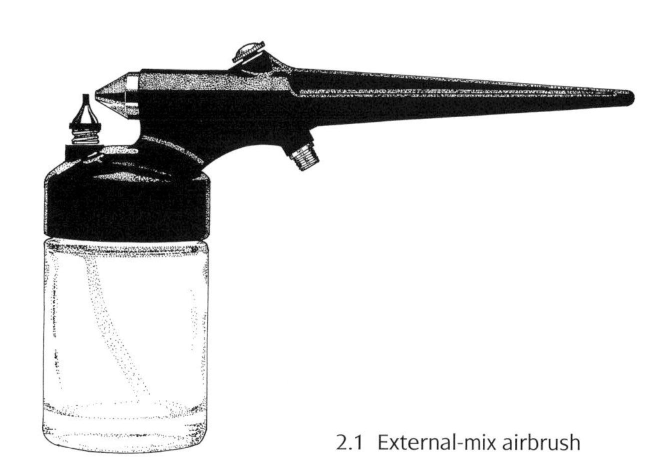

2.1 External-mix airbrush

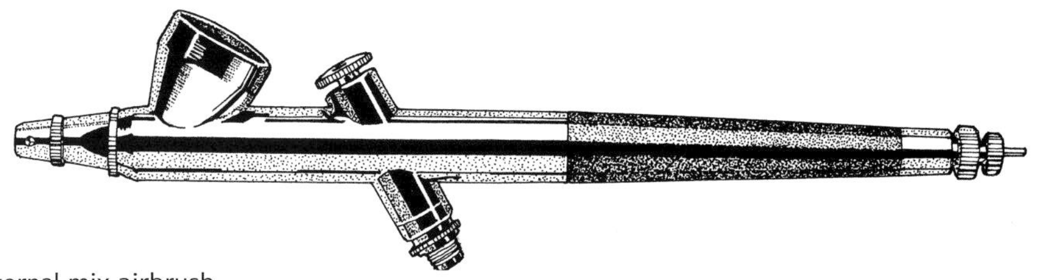

2.2 Internal-mix airbrush

type of airbrush is best for painting backgrounds or for use with thicker, less discriminate painting.

Internal-Mix Airbrushes

The advantage of internal-mix airbrushes (fig. 2.2) is their efficient focusing of air at the airbrush nozzle. This means there is less need for air pressure and therefore less overspray. Internal-mix airbrushes provide the velvety-smooth spraytones, photographlike fades, and ultrafine lines that are the hallmarks of the airbrush medium.

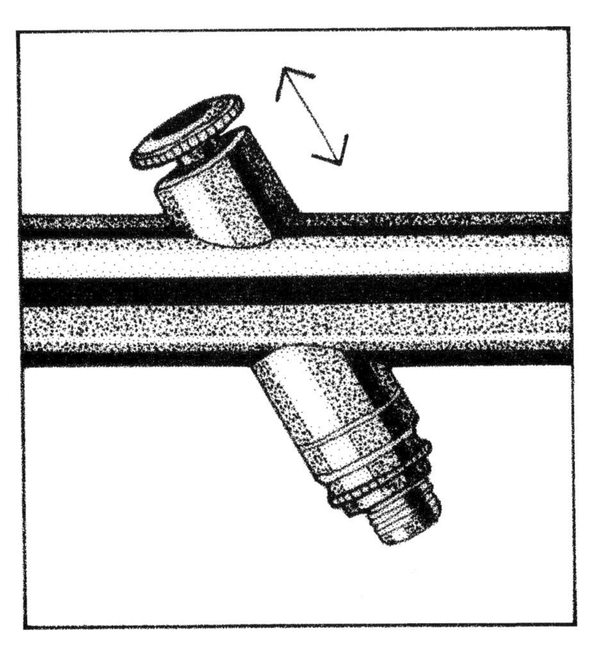

2.3 Single-action trigger

Single-Action Airbrushes

Single-action airbrushes can be either external-mix or internal-mix. The internal-mix version incorporates a needle that provides high-quality spray results. Like all external-mix airbrushes, single-action internal-mix airbrushes use a paint reservoir mounted above, below, or to the side of the handset. The operator uses one simple action during spraying—that is, depression of the trigger that governs the airflow (fig. 2.3). However, when the flow of paint needs to be altered, the operator must stop spraying, loosen the screw at the back of the handset, and readjust the needle, turning it clockwise for a smaller spray pattern and counterclockwise for a larger spray pattern.

Dual-Action Airbrushes

Dual-action internal-mix airbrushes are the type used by the majority of artists and illustrators. Depending upon the model, they can be gravity-fed (with a color cup mounted on top or to one side of the handset), or siphon-fed (with a jar or color cup mounted below the handset). The siphon-feed system tends to be used by artists who fill the siphon jar with stock colors and continuously work in the same color. Gravity-fed airbrushes are used by artists and illustrators who work with small amounts of different colors.

Operating the dual-action airbrush involves two basic maneuvers: pressing down on the trigger to release the air supply and pulling back on the trigger to regulate the volume of paint being sprayed (fig. 2.4). The immediate advantage of this double-function control is that, on most models, the user can, using finger-touch control, modify the width of the spray pattern from a hairline up to a 2-inch-wide pass without stopping. For instance, depressing the trigger and pulling it back slightly introduces a small amount of pigment to the airflow, which results in a narrow stream of fine spray. By keeping the trigger depressed and pulling it back about halfway, you achieve a medium spray suitable for general-purpose work. By pulling the control lever all the way back, you get a wide-angled spray pattern useful for larger spraytones. The spring-loaded action of the control lever means that, when released, it will automatically return to the off position.

We strongly recommend that serious beginners consider investing in the dual-action internal-mix airbrush. The fact that the designer remains in total and uninterrupted control throughout the spraying operation is an advantage that outweighs the airbrush's slightly higher cost.

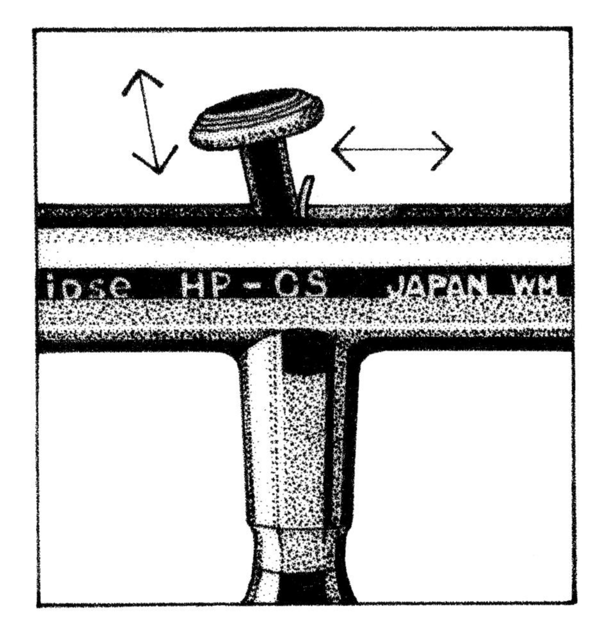

2.4 Dual-action trigger

One of the most reliable airbrush models for architectural illustration is the HP-CS from the Iwata Eclipse Series (fig. 2.5). Priced at around $160, this gravity-feed airbrush comes with a .35 mm needle and nozzle combination, as well as a ⅓ oz. (10 ml) top-mounted color cup that allows the user to work without hindrance close to the artwork surface. The funnel design of the cup makes for easy cleanup and a more efficient paint flow. From time to time, needles and other minor parts may need replacing, but with proper maintenance, this model will give you excellent service (see appendix C).

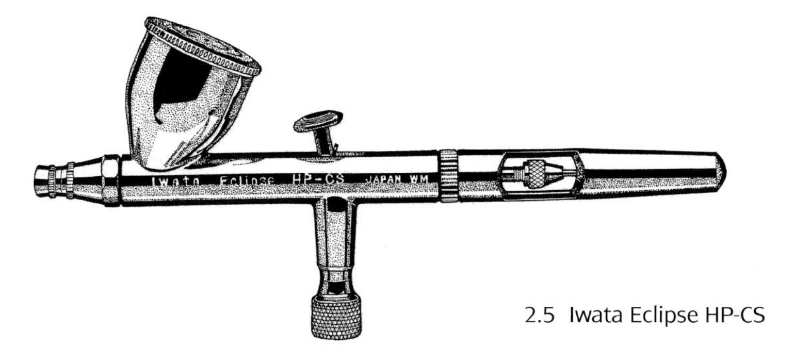

2.5 Iwata Eclipse HP-CS

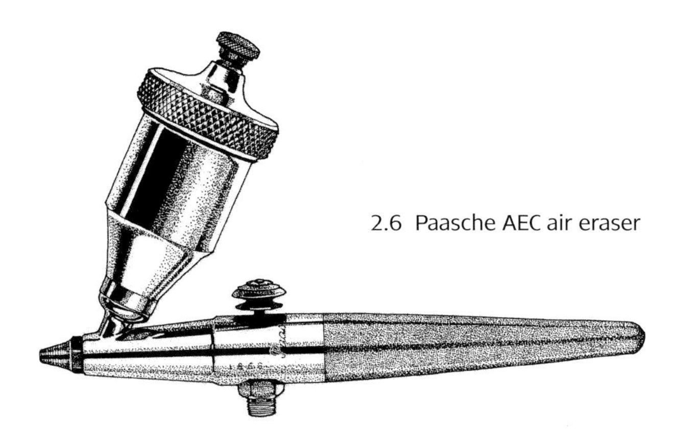

2.6 Paasche AEC air eraser

Air Eraser

A useful but not essential tool is the Paasche AEC Air Eraser (fig. 2.6). This is a versatile instrument priced at around $50. In addition to erasing unwanted areas of spray, it is useful for the introduction of highlights (see page 104). Used only when the artwork is completely dry, the eraser operates with great accuracy, rather like a miniature sandblaster, blowing a jet of fine cutting compound made from cornstarch or pumice. **Caution**: As the fine mist can fill the air, it is recommended that the air eraser be operated outdoors.

Hoses

Airbrush hoses come in two types: linear and coiled. We recommend the coiled version, known as the Cobra (fig. 2.7) because its ability to contract and expand easily allows for movements of the body and arm.

2.7 Cobra hose

Compressors

The compressor is the most expensive part of the airbrush equipment chain. There are two basic types of compressors: those with storage tanks and those without storage tanks. There are three types of motors: diaphragm, oil-bath, and piston and valve. However, the most functional aspect of the compressor is its ability to store air, and most of the diaphragm and piston compressors have no storage tanks. These compressor types are inexpensive but tend to be less efficient than the oil-bath when you are working close to the artwork surface, as they produce pulses of spray that make for an uneven color application. The pulsation problem can be resolved by the addition of a storage tank that is automatically filled by the motor.

Another issue is noise. The noisiest compressors—the piston-driven type—are the cheapest. The diaphragm compressors are less noisy although models range from being surprisingly quiet to very noisy. The term "silent compressor" is usually associated with the oil-bath version, which is the most expensive. These compressors use the type of motor usually found in refrigerators. The tanked oil-bath compressors are a major investment, costing between $400 and $800. Consequently, these models, such as Badger's Trillion Air Silent (fig. 2.8) and the SilentAire 50-15 (fig. 2.9), tend to be used mainly used by professional illustrators.

Despite its drawbacks of noisiness and a fixed air pressure, we recommend the Badger Cyclone 180-1 for beginners (fig. 2.10). Priced around $160, this diaphragm compressor is compact,

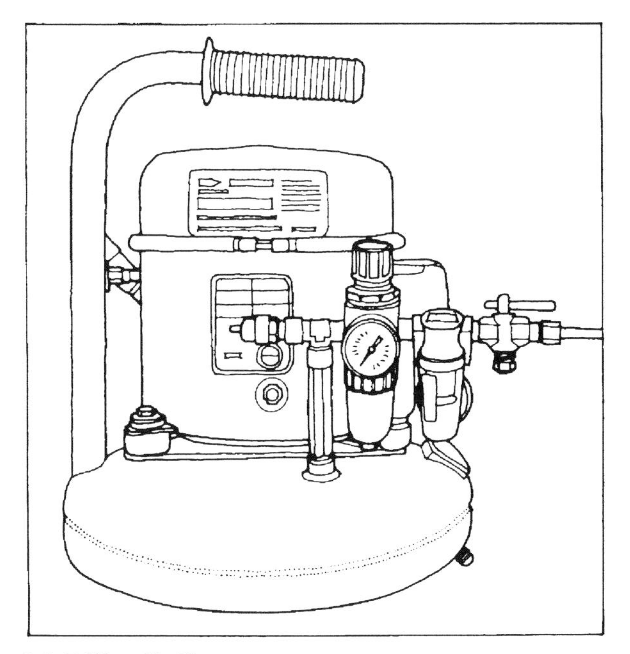

2.8 Trillion Air Silent compressor

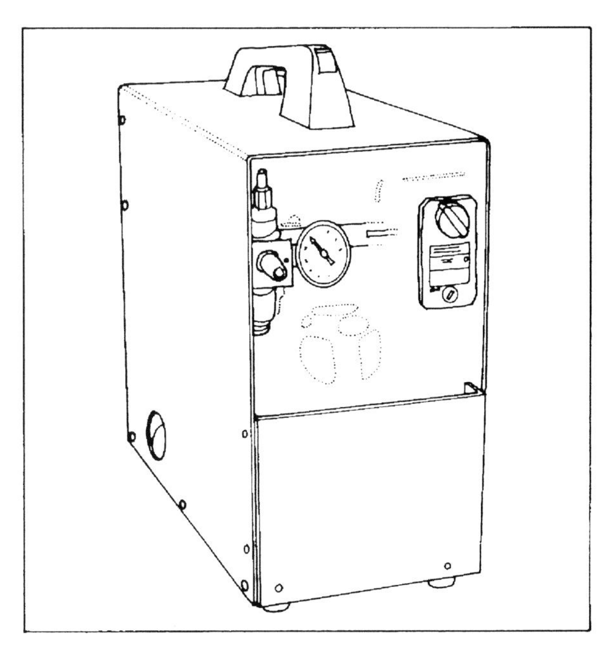

2.9 SilentAire 50-15 compressor

lightweight, and not excessively loud. It is the one used for the majority of the student illustrations in this book.

Note: The airbrush equipment described here can be bought well below list price from specialist mail-order companies. For example, BearAir annually issues *The Airbrush Bible* which offers discounts of up to 75 percent on airbrush equipment.

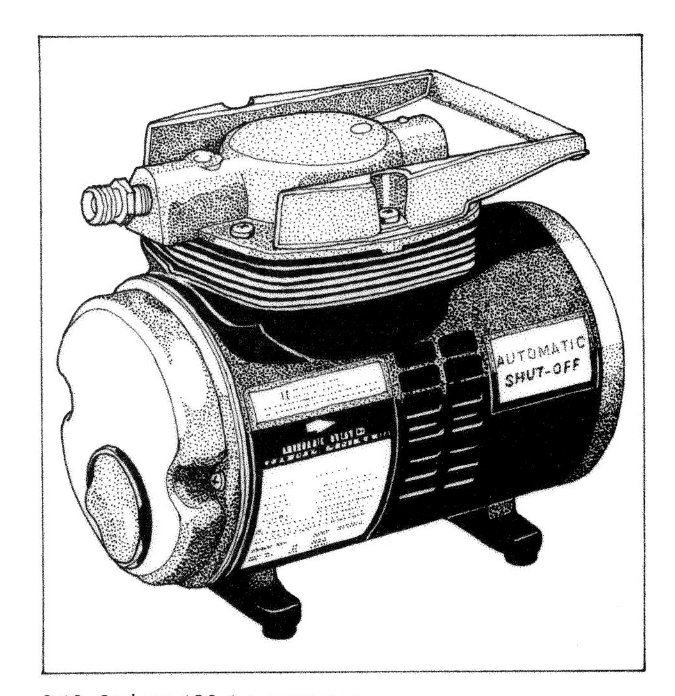

2.10 Cyclone 180-1 compressor

MEDIA

An enormous range of different types of liquid color can be blown through the airbrush, including oil paint, acrylic paint, cellulose paint, lacquers, inks, watercolor, and photographic dyes. (Photographic dyes were used in the early days of professional airbrushing to retouch photographs prior to reproduction. Interestingly, one of the early exponents of this technique was Le Corbusier, who, following his purist principles, is known to have airbrushed out all evidence of nearby buildings in black and white photographs of his built architecture.)

In order to achieve the milky consistency required by the airbrush, many pigments must be diluted before use. Several paints demand special mediums for their dilution, such as white spirit for oil paint, and special solvents for cleaning the airbrush. Furthermore, if the dilution and airbrush cleaning process are not rigorously carried out, some of these pigments can cause clogging during spray application or corrosion of the airbrush itself. For example, inks, although available in a premixed form and luminous in color, present a real drawback. Being shellac-based, they dry extremely hard and must be flushed out of the airbrush immediately after use. Moreover, being similar in nature to dye, they are impermanent, causing work to eventually fade, and in some cases, completely disappear!

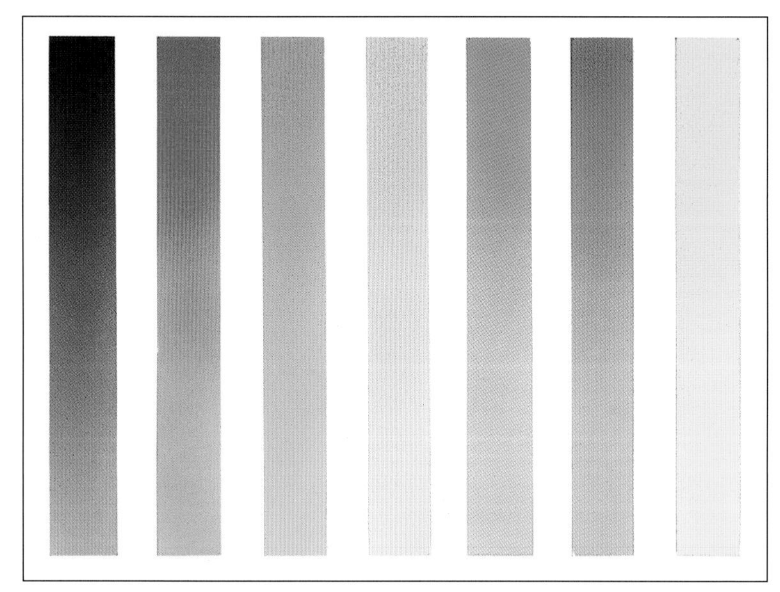

2.11 Starter palette: acrylic

Therefore, although we recommend that you experiment with different types of liquid color, we have chosen to focus on two water-based airbrush paints widely used in architectural illustration. The first, acrylic, is premixed and purchased in a ready-to-use form. The second, watercolor, requires preparatory mixing. Both, however, provide excellent results.

Acrylic

Acrylic paint is plastic-based medium that has been developed into a ready-mixed form specifically for the airbrush. It dries to a durable, permanent, waterproof finish. Among the best-known brands is Golden Artist Colors, Inc., which offers over thirty different hues in transparent or opaque—the latter being a denser version of the color. Another set is manufactured by Iwata-Medea, Inc. under the brand name Medea-ComArt colors. These are also available in transparent and opaque and are offered in containers fitted with dispensers. The properties of Medea-ComArt paint are quite remarkable. Although it is acrylic, and touch-dry when sprayed, it remains water-soluble and workable like watercolor for up to two hours, at which point the paint transforms chemically, or crosslinks, into a waterproof, light-fast acrylic.

Although these acrylics can be used without additives, some paint surfaces, especially highly absorbent surfaces, require acrylic flow release—an additive that increases the fluidity of the paint. We recommend Golden's Flow Release No. 03590.

If you choose acrylic as your airbrush medium, the color selection shown in fig. 2.11 from the Medea-ComArt range (or a comparable palette) is suggested as a basic starter palette: Black, Transparent Rose, Transparent Burnt Orange, Transparent Ochre, Transparent Royal Blue, Transparent Forest Green, Transparent Yellow.

Watercolor

Watercolor is the other recommended airbrush medium. When purchased in tube form, it must be diluted using three parts water to one part pigment. Watercolors provide an unrivaled brilliance, transparency, and, most important, permanence of color. The high quality of this pigment, its potential delicacy of hue, and its extensive color range have made watercolor a top airbrush medium. The majority of the illustrations in this book were produced using Winsor & Newton or HK Holbein transparent artist's quality watercolor. The starter palette shown in fig. 2.12 is drawn from Winsor & Newton's artist's quality range: Lamp Black, Payne's Gray, Cadmium Red, Burnt Sienna, Cerulean Blue, Permanent Sap Green, Cadmium Yellow Pale.

Another professional quality watercolor that is also recommended is produced by M. Graham & Co. Since this range is made with honey, the paint is prevented from hardening either on the palette or in the tube and will easily dilute—even after months of disuse.

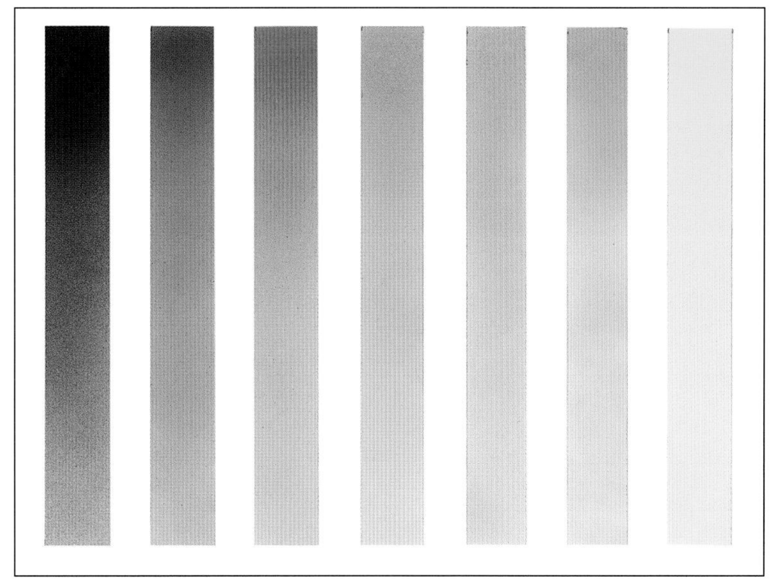

2.12 Starter palette: watercolor

SURFACES

The range of potential surfaces for the airbrush medium is limited only by the designer's imagination. However, the type of surface selected for a particular work is just as important as the choice of liquid color. This is because different surfaces have different qualities and characteristics that greatly affect the final appearance of the airbrushed image. Generally speaking, acrylics and watercolor pigments work best on good-quality papers and boards.

It is important that the surface be durable enough to withstand the use of masking tape and frisket film (an adhesive-backed film used to protect areas of the image during spraying; see chapter 4 for an in-depth description). Cold-Pressed (CP) Crescent illustration board No. 110, and Arches rough (R) 300 lb (640 g) watercolor paper are good choices. We recommend that watercolor paper be at least 300 lb, as weights less than 140 lb (300 g) tend to buckle when airbrush spray is combined with paint-brush-applied color. (If the lighter-weight paper does buckle, after being sprayed, the undulations can easily be removed by dampening the back of the paper with a clean, moist sponge. Take care not to allow any moisture to run over the edge of the paper and creep under to damage the illustration. Then protect the artwork with clean paper before placing it face down on a flat surface. Cover the back of the watercolor paper with a board, weight it down with stacks of books, and leave it to dry naturally. The pressure will return it to its original flatness.) Unless stated otherwise, these surfaces are recommended for all the exercises outlined in this book.

Although watercolor paper provides a tough surface that withstands the rigors of treatments used to create textural effects, illustration board is more commonly used. Illustration board manufacturers produce one type designed specifically for airbrushing. Because they look similar to other types, it is important to purchase them by name and designation. We recommend the Frisk C.S. 10 illustration board, which is manufactured in the United Kingdom and available in the U.S., and touted as "the original supreme line surface board."

THE WORKSPACE

You can airbrush almost anywhere—any room or space of adequate size can be quickly converted into an airbrush studio. Ideally, you should have ready access to a clean water supply, but plastic squeeze bottles can be used if a water source is not available. Before setting up the space there are some basic but crucial points that must be addressed. First and foremost is the need for adequate ventilation. This aspect of airbrushing cannot be overstressed. The airbrush emits invisible particles of atomized pigment that remain airborne, and long exposure to spraying in an unventilated space can produce a serious health hazard. An open window or door, preferably both, to provide a cross-draft, allows fresh air to circulate. Also, we strongly advise the use of a respirator, or surgical mask. Avoid spraying for extensive periods of time, and avoid airbrushing in excessively humid conditions, as too much moisture in the atmosphere can create an unhealthy environment as well as adversely affect the smooth spraying action of the airbrush. A final word of caution: Keep both the artwork and the equipment spotlessly clean and free from contamination. Never bring food or drink into the studio space.

The chosen workspace should be well lit, preferably by sunlight, although this is not essential. If you choose to work in electric light, remember that colors will appear slightly—or sometimes radically—different under different light sources. This is because some illuminants, such as tungsten, emit a warm, yellowish light, while many fluorescents provide a cool, bluish light. It is often helpful to use a mix of different types of light sources. For example, you could light the artwork surface with a tungsten lamp while using overhead fluorescent light.

If you use transparencies as the basis

for artwork, it is useful to have the ability to black out the studio space. Tracing a slide-projected image in the studio is preferable, though not crucial, to having to conduct this transfer process elsewhere.

Your workspace ideally should also incorporate an electricity supply to power the compressor and other equipment, such as a projector. If this is not possible, compressed air can be imported from aerosol air canisters or from an inflated car-tire inner tube attached to the hose via an adaptor.

The studio should contain a table, bench, desk, or any flat surface to serve as the base for your airbrush easel. You can make an inexpensive, portable easel (fig. 2.13) from a sheet of ½ in (13 mm) plywood cut to a size of 24 x 32 in (61 x 81 cm). Sand its edges and cut a triangular prop from the same material, with one side cut at a 15-degree angle to the vertical. Once this is sanded, attach the angled edge along the center of the back of the easel using two 1½ in (4 cm) hinges. Finally, assemble an L-shaped ledge with a ¾ in (2 cm) reveal to secure the artwork from two strips of 1 x 1½ in (2.5 x 4 cm) wood. Once it is sanded and screw-attached to the bottom edge of the work surface, seal the easel front and back with two coats of polyurethane to prevent warping and allow for ease of cleaning.

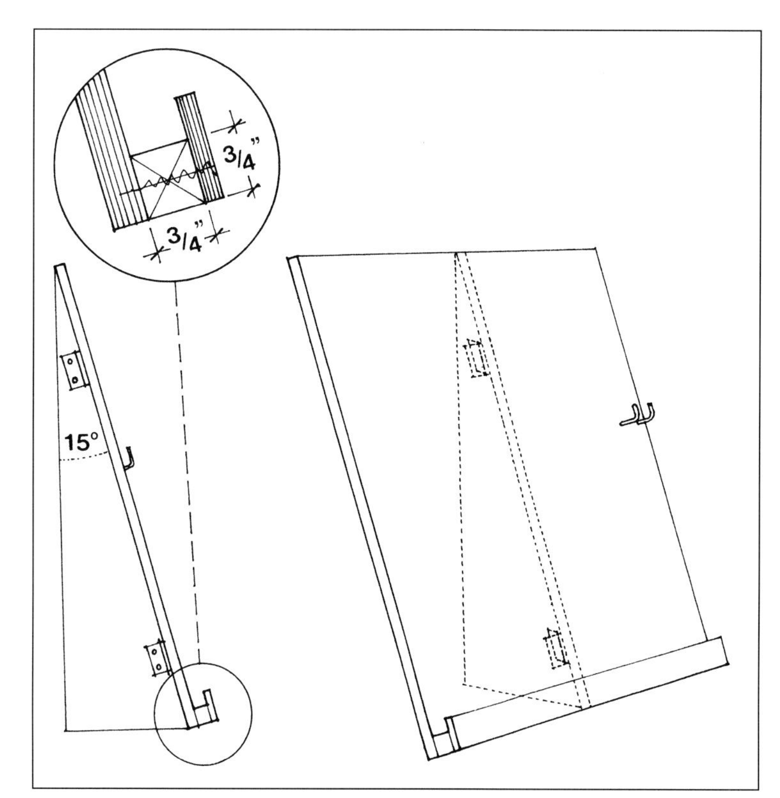

2.13 Do-it-yourself airbrush easel

You can also attach a carrying handle to the top of the easel and two metal L hooks to one side of the work surface to hold the handset when not in use. Position the L hooks by holding the airbrush against the surface of the easel and marking the appropriate points.

The serious airbrusher can make a more permanent workstation that obviates the need for tables. George Dombek constructed a wall-mounted timber lattice grid assembled from 8 in (20 cm) lengths of ¼ x ¾ in (6 x 20 mm) strips of wood. Mounted on battens to keep proud of the wall, the structure acts as a grid on which to hang the drawing board in any desired work position. When hung, the board can be tilted outward at its base using a short length of wood; the weight of the board holds the prop in position (fig. 2.14).

In addition to the necessary equipment of airbrush and compressor, paint, paper, and illustration board, you will need drafting tape, frisket film (available in sheet and roll form in most good art-supply shops), a metal straightedge,

2.14 George Dombek's wall-mounted easel

and an X-Acto knife with a No. 11 blade (complete with spares). Several items should be kept near at hand—pencils, including a 4H lead for drawing, scalpels for general-purpose cutting, a paintbrush for mixing colors, and an eraser. It is also good practice to keep an abundant supply of clean cloths that do not shed lint, and paper tissues for cleaning. You will also need lots of scraps of paper and cardstock for use as supplementary masks, for rehearsing rendering techniques, and for the preliminary testing of spraytones before airbrushing directly onto the artwork. A mixing palette is also essential—you can use a white dinner plate or a sheet of glass placed over a piece of white paper.

CONNECTING THE EQUIPMENT

The first task is to connect the hose to your airbrush and to the compressor. If the hose has screw-fitting couplings, simply turn until an airtight seal is formed. It is a good idea to first wrap all the threads with white plumber's tape, as this helps to achieve an airtight seal. Another type of connection—fitted as an adaptor—is the quick-connect coupling. This push-fit type is useful for illustrators who use more than one type of airbrush.

Before proceeding it is wise to check for air leaks at each connection. When not using a preset compressor, you can do this by setting the pressure regulator to the standard operating pressure of 30 psi before depressing the airbrush control level all the way down to release a test jet of air.

All compressors and hoses, to an extent, leak air. If you are using a tanked compressor and the pump automatically cuts in more than once per hour, there is an air leak somewhere in the system. Usually this occurs from the connections at either end of the hose.

Some basic airbrush exercises show how to handle and maintain the airbrush, and represent the first important steps in airbrush illustration, the subject of chapter 3.

3 On Your Marks: Dots, Lines, and Spraytones

It is now time to familiarize yourself with the airbrush. Hold it comfortably as if it were a traditional fat-barreled pen—i.e., between your thumb and second finger with your forefinger resting on top of the control lever (fig. 3.1). There is no set rule for handling the airbrush but it is important that it feels right for you while you maintain forefinger command over the control lever.

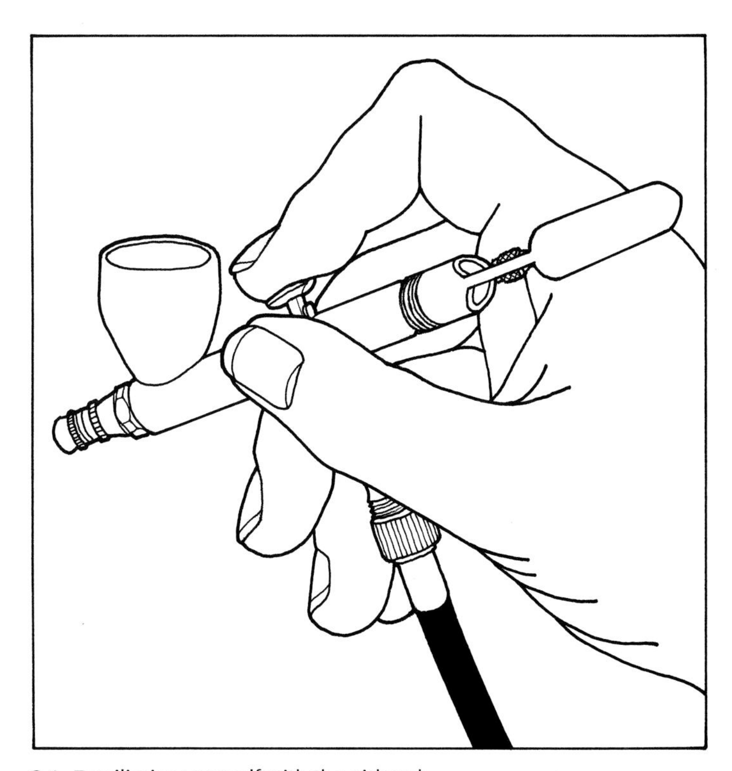

3.1 Familiarize yourself with the airbrush.

TAKING CONTROL

Before introducing paint into the reservoir, practice some of the basic airbrush control actions. For example, press the trigger down to release the air supply (this action is always good practice before loading the color cup, as it ensures that the brush is free from dust and moisture). Now depress the trigger again, but this time keep the lever depressed and pull it slowly backward. This introduces the flow of air to the paint supply. Releasing the control lever allows it to spring back into its original position, which automatically shuts

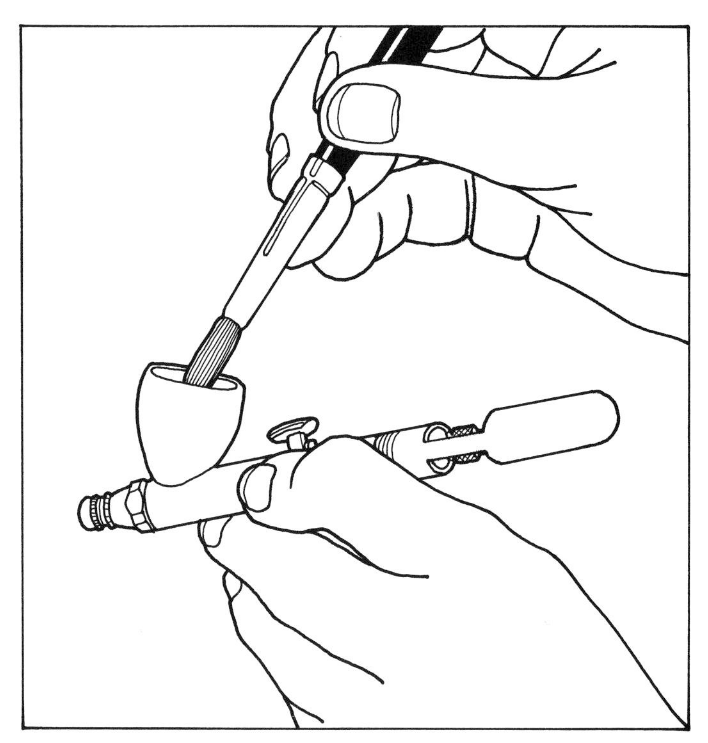

3.2 Transferring the paint to the color cup

down the flow of compressed air and paint.

This is the main airbrush action. The more you practice it, the easier it will be to control the airbrush while working. Therefore, invest a little time in practicing these basic operations before you fill the color cup. The aim is to develop a degree of confidence with the airbrush and its controls. Rehearsing these dry maneuvers will help you get used to the airbrush as a natural extension of your hand and eye.

When you feel confident enough and ready for the real thing, you can undertake some basic exercises. First make sure that your hands are clean. Then mount a sheet of inexpensive paper, such as bond paper or butcher paper, on your easel.

Mixing the Paint and Loading the Color Cup

If you are using a premixed paint, release the dispenser cap and pour a small amount of black paint directly into the airbrush color cup. If you are working with watercolor, squeeze about ⅛ in (3 mm) of lampblack paint into a jar and, using a clean paintbrush, thoroughly mix with three parts water to achieve the creamy consistency of milk. Then transfer the paint to the color cup using the paintbrush (fig. 3.2). Avoid spilling the paint—whether acrylic or watercolor—on the body or head of the airbrush. If this does occur, wipe away any excess paint with a clean cloth or tissue.

Common mistakes made by beginners using watercolor are to overdilute the mixture (causing too light a spraytone), underdilute the mixture (inhibiting the flow of pigment in the airbrush), or mix an excessive quantity of paint. The internal-mix airbrush is equipped with a very small color cup and requires only a small quantity of pigment. Aim to underfill the color cup. This will avoid accidental spillage during airbrushing, and you will be surprised at the vast area that this thimble-sized amount of pigment will cover.

THE BASIC EXERCISES: DOTS, LINES, AND SPRAYTONES

Before embarking on the four following basic mark-making exercises, test the airbrush operation. This prelude is intended not only to test the function of the airbrush and the paint but also to help you loosen up.

From about 4 in (10 cm) away, aim the airbrush at the paper and press down on the trigger to release the air. Then gently pull the trigger backward to release the paint into the jetstream for a random spray. Experience the feel of the airbrush in your hand, practice the forefinger-operated on and off action, and rehearse the coordination of your hand and eye. This warm-up session is also helpful for checking the consistency of the spray pattern.

Once you feel reasonably happy with the controls and the appearance of the spray pattern, mount another sheet of bond or butcher paper on the easel and try the following exercise.

Exercise 1 **Dots**

Hold the airbrush in a relaxed manner, keeping it perpendicular to the surface of the artwork and at a distance of 4–5 in (10–13 cm) from the paper. With your hand perfectly still, press down on the trigger and gently pull back to release a jet of spray. Follow this by making a series of quick-burst dots on the paper (fig. 3.3).

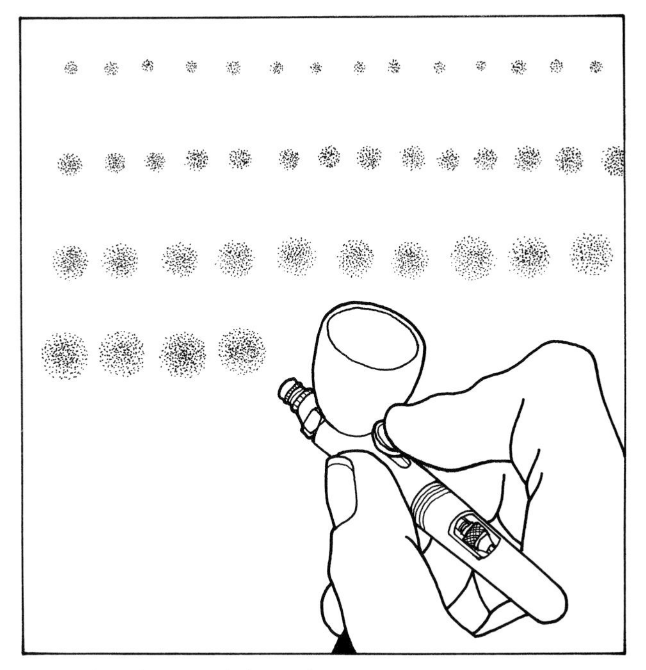

3.3 Airbrushing quick-burst dots

Next, try producing dots of spray from different spraying distances. Start at ¼ in (0.5 cm) away from the paper and incrementally increase the distance until you are 5 in (13 cm) away. You will quickly notice that the nearer the airbrush nozzle is to the paper, the smaller, crisper, and more concentrated the paint pattern will be (fig. 3.4). Spend some time with this exercise until you feel confident enough to attempt a second airbrush maneuver.

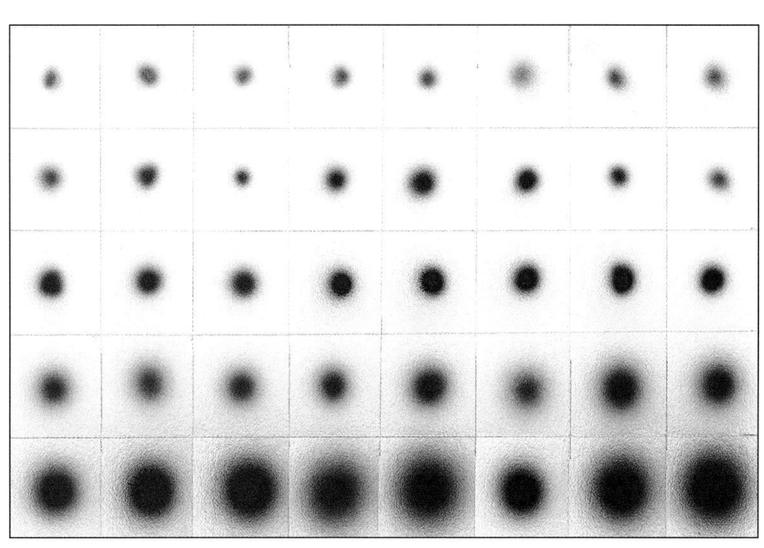

3.4 Student exercise: Dots of various sizes

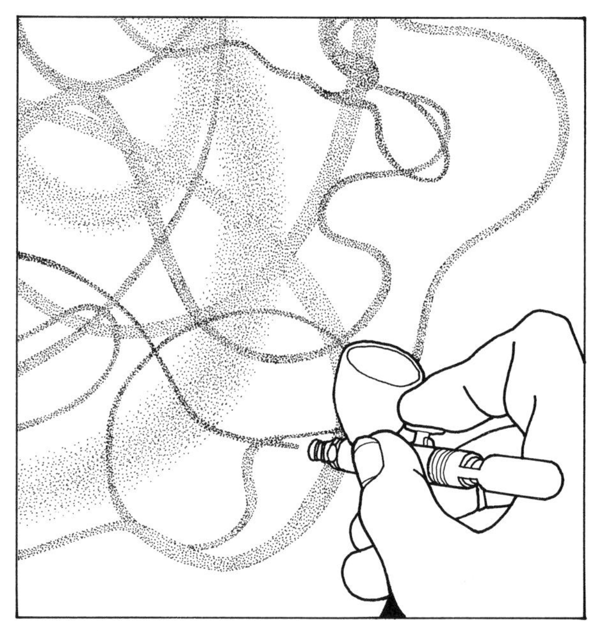

3.5 Snaking lines of various widths

3.6 Student exercise: Snaking lines

Exercise 2 **Lines**

Now adopt a more playful approach. Try making a continuous, snaking line over the entire width of the paper (fig. 3.5). At the beginning of the line, keep the airbrush head close to the paper and then gradually move away. See how thin you can make the line and then how thick it can become. Continue by making several meandering, pulsating lines across the paper (fig. 3.6).

Now try producing some straight lines, but this time use both hands, allowing your free hand to rest on the surface of the paper while cupping and supporting the hand controlling the airbrush. Move across the paper while aiming to create a perfectly straight line (fig. 3.7). This sliding, two-handed spraying technique affords you more control for precise work. Try producing a series of lines of different quality by varying the distance between the paper and the airbrush (fig. 3.8). An alternative method of producing perfectly straight lines is to rest the airbrush nozzle on a tilted straightedge placed directly on the surface of the artwork.

Experimenting with these dot and line exercises will help you learn not only basic airbrush control but also something about the limitations and abilities of your particular airbrush model. For instance, some airbrushes will work as close as ½ in (1 cm) from the paper and as far back as 8–9 in (20–23 cm). Compressors also affect the distance you can achieve; compressors preset at 30 psi do not allow the airbrush to produce fine lines at very close range.

Exercise 3 **Even Spraytones**

The third exercise introduces what the airbrush can do better than any other paint-application medium—that is, lay down an immaculately flat or gradated spraytone. Before attempting this exercise you will need a piece of cardstock or illustration board mounted on the easel. You also may need to recharge the airbrush color cup.

Note that the airbrush model recommended in chapter 2, although an excellent tool for the production of architectural illustration, is useful primarily for detailed work, as it will only achieve a broad spray pattern approximately 1–2 in (3–5 cm) wide. To produce large areas of even or gradated tone, you would have to turn to other models that allow a broader spray pattern.

Perfectly even and gradated spraytones are, however, achievable with your airbrush. It will take some practice to accomplish the desired result, and you should make as many attempts as necessary to develop this important skill.

To airbrush an area of even value, outline a 4 x 6 in (10 x 15 cm) rectangle with a 4H pencil. Hold the airbrush about 6 or 7 in (15 or 18 cm) away from the surface of the paper, and try to produce an even spraytone within the rectangle. Work from the top of the rectangle, and begin each stroke by spraying from outside its limits. Make a series of horizontal passes, spraying from left to right, and vice versa. It is important to allow each pass to gently overlap the previous one (fig. 3.9). Aim for a light, even tone—apply a minimum of backward pressure on the trigger and use the same trigger setting for each of the strokes.

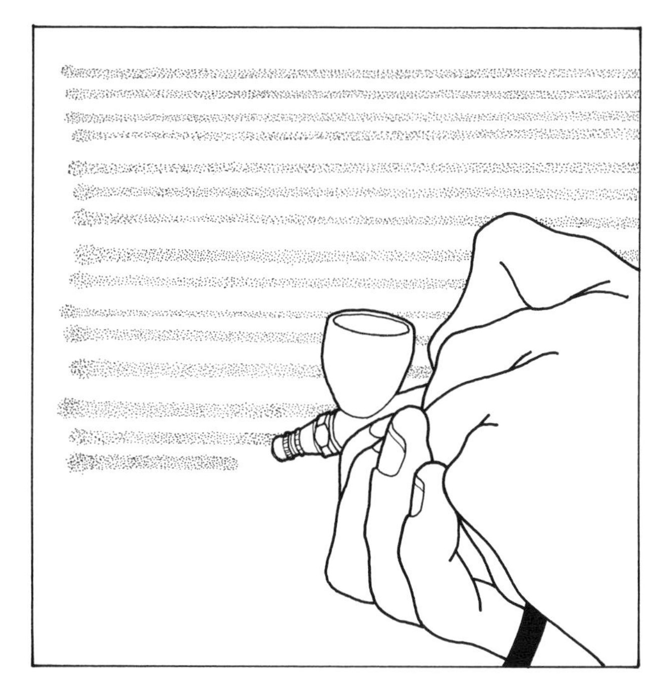

3.7 Airbrushing straight lines

3.8 Student exercise: Various line qualities

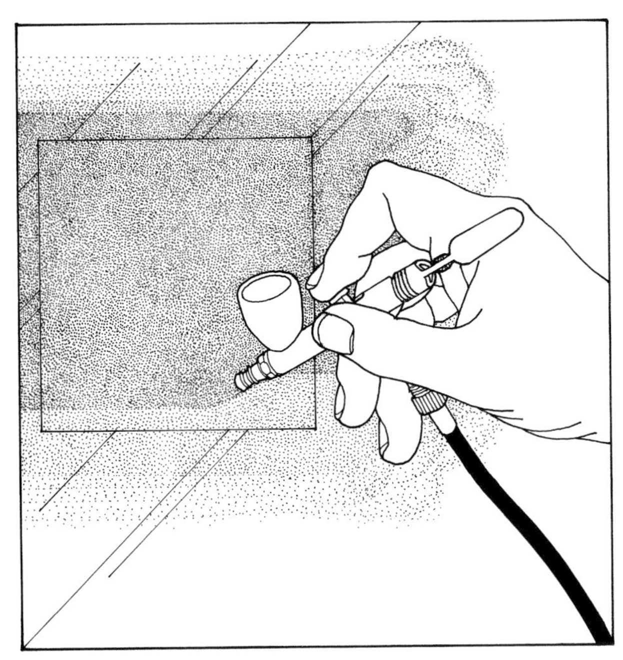

Figure 3.9 Making horizontal passes

Figure 3.10: Student exercise: Even spraytone

As you move down the rectangle, use the overlapping bands of spray to correct any imperfections in previous passes. The finished spraytone will result from a buildup of superimposed spraytones. A light-toned spraytone may require three or four passes, each laid over another across the rectangular format (fig. 3.10). A spraytone of a darker, denser value may take ten or more applications. In order to check the value effect of multilayered passes, examine the chart in figure 3.11. This chart results from nine passes over a grid of successively exposed squares, the top-left square showing the depth of value achieved from all nine passes.

In order to examine the evenness of your final spraytone, cut out the airbrushed rectangle and place it on a sheet of white paper. If your first attempt at an even spraytone appears patchy, do a series of vertical passes to even it out. Continue making both light and dark spraytone versions of this exercise until you have completely mastered this technique.

Exercise 4 **Gradated Spraytones**

It might seem logical to create a spraytone fade by using three settings of the airbrush trigger to spray three connected bands of value: dark, mid-gray, and light, fusing the three value layers into a gradated fade. However, it is almost impossible to achieve a seamless fade using this method. Using the same trigger setting throughout the spraying operation provides a better means of achieving a gradated spraytone. This approach forms the basis of this exercise.

Begin the gradated fade with an initial light, even, but solid spraytone that is airbrushed in overlapping passes to completely fill an outlined 4 x 6 in (10 x 15 cm) rectangle. Then begin a second layer of spraytone starting at the top and working in horizontal passes downward while spraying a consistent application of the same value. However, this time terminate the spraytone approximately 1 in (3 cm) short of the lower edge (fig. 3.12). Continue by repeating these passes, stopping each spraytone about an inch above the previous spraytone. This technique allows you to create very professional-looking fade effects (fig. 3.13).

These four techniques are an essential part of the airbrush repertoire. In particular, mastering even and gradated spraytones is key to successful airbrushing, and it is vital that you practice them until you feel confident in your ability to achieve them.

3-11: Value chart resulting from nine passes over successively exposed squares

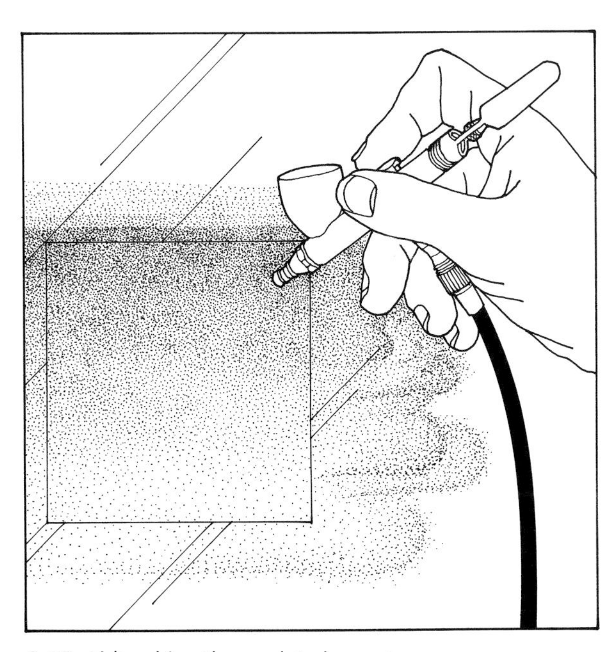

3-12 Airbrushing the gradated spraytone

3.13 Student exercise: Gradated spraytone

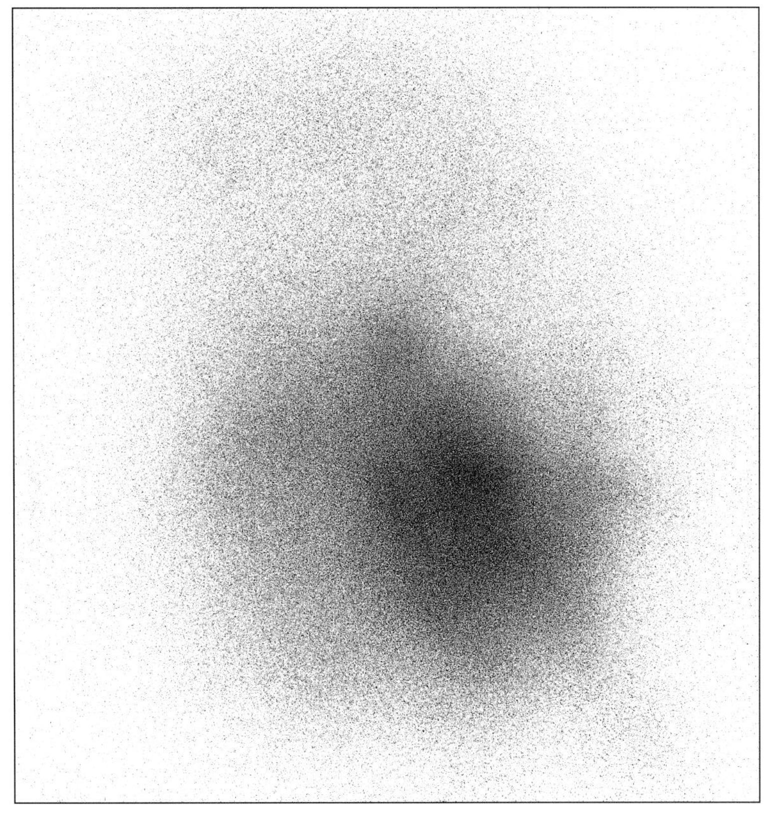

3.14 Spatter effect

Exercise 5 Spatter Effect

Spatter (fig. 3.14) provides a coarse-grained effect that is often employed as a visual contrast to the smooth spraytone traditionally associated with the airbrush. The effect is similar to that achieved by traditional watercolor painters when they scrape a piece of card or their forefinger against the paint-loaded bristles of an old toothbrush aimed at the paper. Spatter is achieved by removing the needle cap and nozzle cap at the front of the airbrush (see appendix C). Another method on some models is to interrupt the air supply during the spraying operation by sealing the reservoir with the thumb. Also, if your compressor is preset at 30 psi, you will have already discovered that a stipple effect is caused by holding the airbrush very close to the surface of the artwork. If the compressor is fitted with an air regulator, a spatter effect may be achieved by reducing the pressure to between 5 and 10 psi. There is also a specially manufactured spatter-cap attachment that can be fitted to the head of some airbrush models.

The ability to create spatter effects depends on the airbrush model—for instance, the Iwata HP-CS is designed to produce a wide range of stippling textures. A few models, such as Holbein's Dash Y-2 B3145, have an adjustable head. Turning it clockwise reduces the dot pattern to a very fine spray. Turning it counterclockwise opens up the nozzle to create a heavy dot pattern. As different airbrush models create spatter effects using different means, it is important that you consult the manual for your specific model.

When used in conjunction with even or gradated spraytones, the potential of this effect can be quite magnificent. In addition, while it achieves interesting optical textural effects, the spatter pattern reveals the very essence of the airbrush technique.

These initial exercises may seem simplistic, but they are a fundamental part of mastering the airbrush medium. Spend as much time as you can exploring and expanding this basic vocabulary of marks, as well as mentally noting the actions that produced them.

CLEANING THE AIRBRUSH

At the end of each airbrushing session or if the airbrush has been unused for a long period of time, it is good practice to thoroughly clean it. Different types of airbrushes require different cleaning regimens. For example, the needle of an external-mix airbrush will dry out in just fifteen minutes (leading to serious problems), whereas the internal-mix airbrush can be set aside for up to two hours because its needle remains partially submerged in pigment. However, it cannot be stressed enough that if left for extensive periods without being cleaned, your airbrush will suffer irrevocably. It is extremely important to clean the airbrush between each color change and, of course, at the end of each spraying session.

A number of proprietary airbrush cleaning fluids are on the market. They can be purchased in concentrated form and diluted using a ratio of one part solvent to ten parts water. However, you should exercise caution when using these solvents because their fumes can present health hazards. For this reason, we recommend using water as a cleansing agent. However, water will not work as a cleaning fluid for all types of paints. Non-water-based paints, such as oil, lacquer, and cellulose, each require their own cleaning agent.

The best way to clean your airbrush between color changes is to first tip into a sink any residual paint from the color cup and then shoot the remaining paint directly into the flow of cold water from a faucet. Then fill the color cup with clean water and spray it through the airbrush while retracting and depressing the trigger to its full extent. Do this a minimum of three times. The full retraction and depression of the trigger allows the water to pass through the nozzle at its maximum opening. Then wipe out the color cup with a clean cloth.

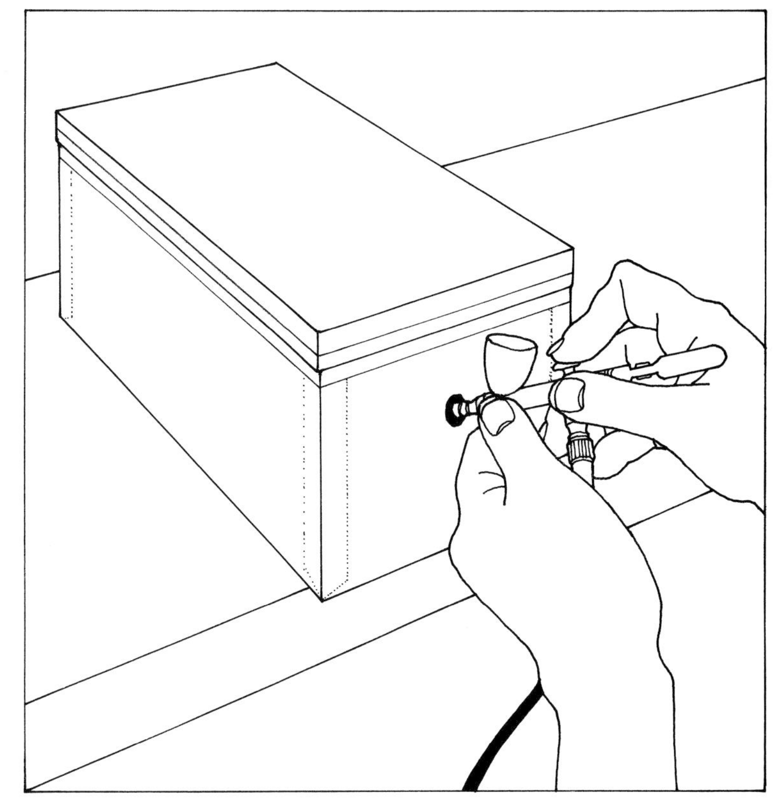

3.15 The do-it-yourself mist control box

Because the cleaning procedure requires you to fully retract and depress the trigger, some spraying of pigment will occur. If you don't have a sink to control such spray, a mist control box should be used. Proprietary mist control boxes can be purchased, but a do-it-yourself version can be easily made from a cardboard box. Half-fill the box with crumpled tissue paper before replacing the lid, and seal the box with tape. Punch a hole the same diameter as the airbrush nozzle in the center of one end. Insert the nozzle into the hole and discharge the contents of the color cup safely into the box (fig. 3.15). To maintain the mist control box's efficiency, occasionally replenish the paint-soiled tissue paper with a new filling.

Before packing away your airbrush at the end of a working session, you must also clean the needle. Remove the tail cap, loosen the needle chucking nut, and slowly pull the needle straight out (see appendix C). Wipe the residue from the needle by gently rotating it in a fold of clean paper tissue. Before returning the needle to its housing, spray some clean water through the airbrush. Then carefully reinsert the needle into the airbrush and push gently until it sits against the nozzle. Screw back the needle chucking nut to lock it into place.

Although this cleaning procedure initially may seem excessive, the routine is vital to the creation of good airbrush illustration—a good craftsperson is only as good as his or her tools. Plus, you have spent considerable money on the equipment, so it makes sense to take good care of it! A well-maintained airbrush can last you a lifetime.

4 Masking Agents and Surface-Pigment Interaction

Central to the airbrushing technique is the masking process. Although a few fine artists work entirely in freehand—that is, without the aid of masks—the vast majority use some form of masking agent to protect the edges of the areas surrounding an exposed shape that is to be sprayed. Masks are also used to provide either sharp or, as shown later, soft edges. There are four basic types of mask in common use: frisket film, drafting tape, liquid masks, and hand-held masks.

FRISKET FILM

Frisket film can be purchased in different materials, but the one made from adhesive-backed acetate has many advantages. Being transparent, it allows you to remain in constant contact with an evolving airbrush image, and being extremely thin, it allows you to cut highly intricate shapes and resists paint creeping under it or building up along its edge. Also, with careful handling, acetate frisket film can be removed and then reused in later stages of an illustration's production.

Frisket film is manufactured in a variety of sheet and roll sizes, but a manageable size is the 20 x 25 in (50 x 63 cm) format. Frisket film comes in three basic grades of tack: high, medium, and low. However, these degrees of tack are not standardized across brands. For instance, what might be designated as high tack in one brand of film will seem medium tack compared to another. Generally speaking, avoid the low-tack friskets, as small pieces of mask, especially in the more delicate areas of an illustration, may flutter away from the surface or be blown away by the airbrush. Also, low-tack frisket tends to lift the edges of the darker, heavier deposits of paint when it is removed.

We recommend two products from the range of available frisket film: Grafix prepared frisket extra-tack film manufactured by Graphic Art Systems, Inc., and high-tack Friskfilm made by Frisk Graphic Art Materials. These are

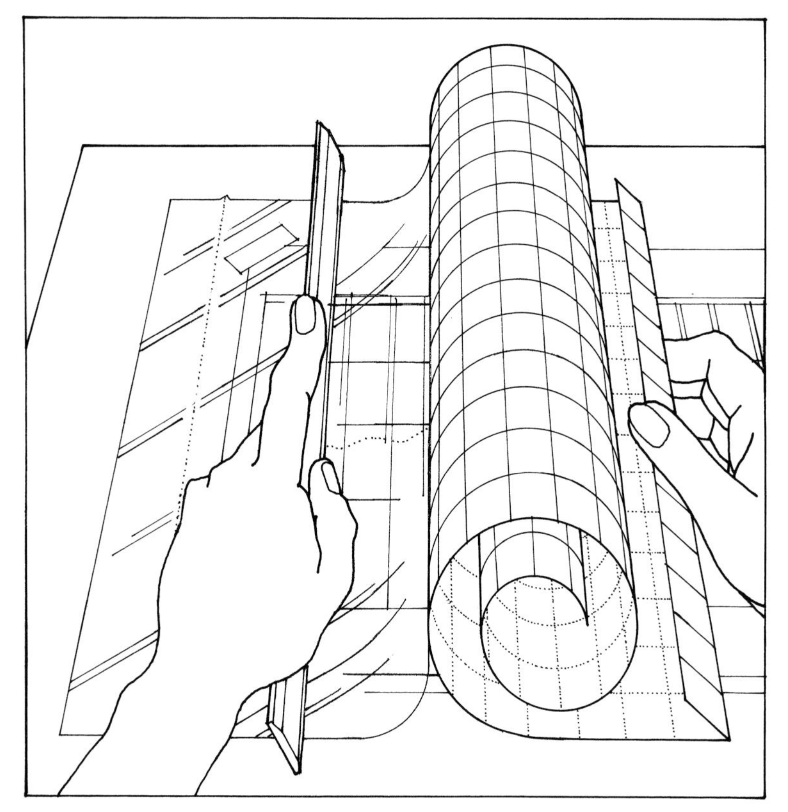

4.1 Applying frisket film to the artwork surface

preferred because they are safe to use on Crescent illustration board No. 110 and on Arches rough watercolor paper. These products don't seem to interfere with the artwork and can be overlaid easily on previously sprayed artwork without damaging the painted surface.

Applying Frisket Film

The masking procedure usually begins after the image to be airbrushed has been drawn on the paper support. Completely cover the outline drawing with frisket film. To apply the film, first separate and pull back about a 1 in (3 cm) strip of sheet backing. Then, after cutting away the released strip of sheet backing, attach the exposed edge of the film to one side of the area to be protected. Next, gently pull and slowly release the sheet backing from behind until it is removed from the back of the film. At the same time, with the other hand press the edge of a ruler or triangle on the face of the frisket and, maintaining firm pressure, track the line of its separation (fig. 4.1). If a bubble occurs, puncture it with the point of the X-Acto blade and then burnish it down with your forefinger.

To cover larger areas with frisket, apply several sheets in a mosaic fashion, allowing them to slightly overlap at all connecting edges. Even when overlapped, the film is thin enough to be cut through.

When using watercolor paper, illustrators traditionally paint all the way to the edges of the paper. With illustration board, it is traditional to leave a white (unpainted) border around the airbrushed image. Thus, with illustration board it is economical to use frisket film only on the airbrushed illustration itself and apply a secondary mask made of scraps of clean paper to the outer edge of the board. Attach this outer mask to the board with drafting tape, with the inner edges of the tape forming the boundary of the airbrushed area (fig. 4.2).

Cutting Frisket Film

Mask cutting is one of the most important phases in airbrushing. It requires a very sharp X-Acto blade. After the frisket film is laminated to the drawing surface, carefully trace-cut all the lines of the drawing beneath it. In other words, redraw the image, but this time with the knife blade. Take great care to cut through only the film and not the paper or board below. Sensing just the right amount of pressure needed to successfully trace-cut the mask without damaging the underlying surface is an acquired skill; it is a delicate operation that can only be mastered through trial and error. Therefore, it is wise to spend some time making practice cuts on trial pieces of frisket-laminated paper and board (fig. 4.3).

A good way of developing the delicate touch required for frisket-film cutting is to simply rest the point of the knife blade on the surface of the film and trace the line—in other words, don't apply any pressure at all. Try several trial cuts like this to see just how little pressure is needed.

Cutting all the lines and shapes in a drawing before airbrushing allows for an uninterrupted airbrushing stage. However, more complicated illustrations may require you to alternate cutting and spraying—that is, cut only a portion of the drawing, expose and spray it, remask it with the frisket (to protect it from subsequent spray), then cut another portion, expose and spray it, remask it, and so on. This procedure is a little more difficult, as the lines of the drawing may gradually obscure under subsequent layers of overspray, making the later cutting stages difficult, if not impossible. Another problem with this technique is replacing the frisket. Frisket film, especially on complicated shapes, is notoriously difficult to accurately replace. When this situation arises, it is often easier to cut a new frisket for the area. Generally, whenever possible, conduct the frisket-cutting stage in

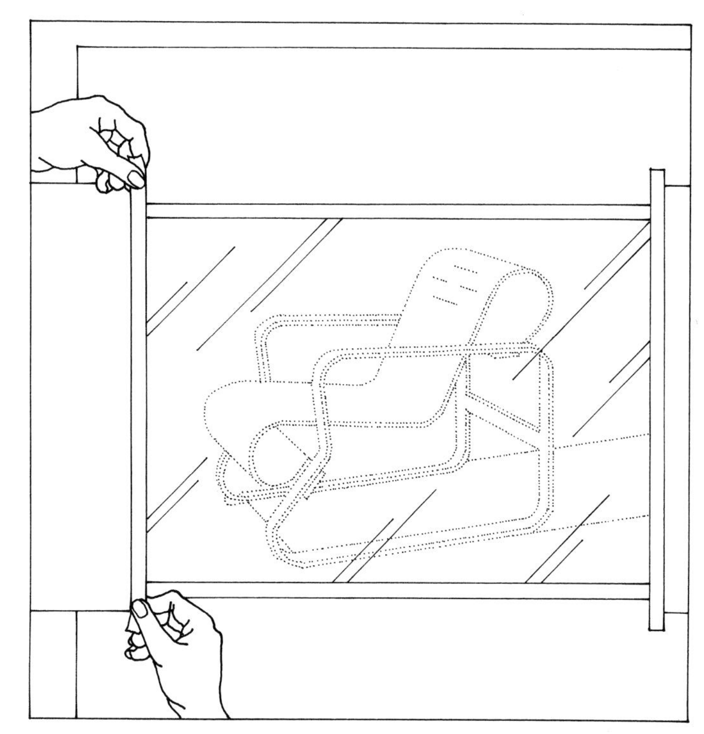

4.2 Economizing on frisket film

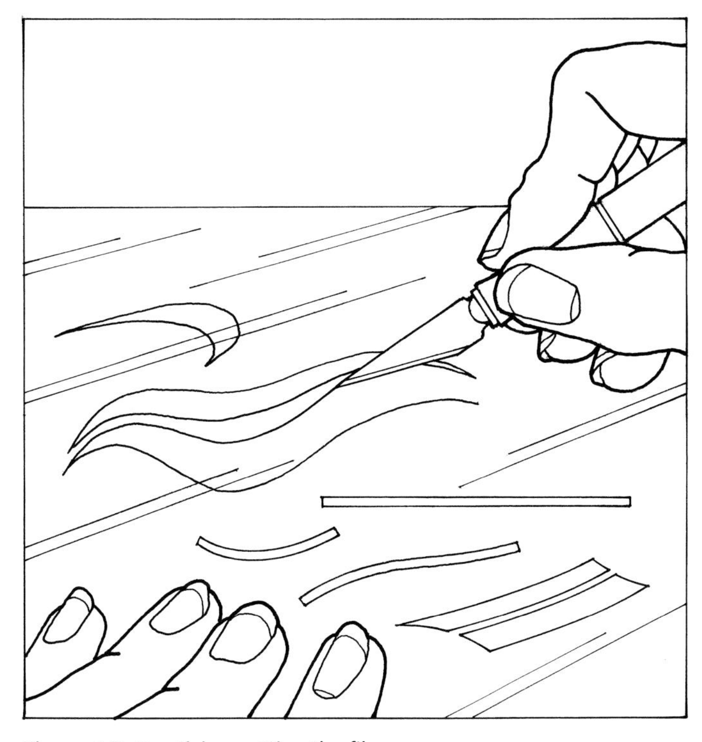

Figure 4.3 Practicing cutting the film

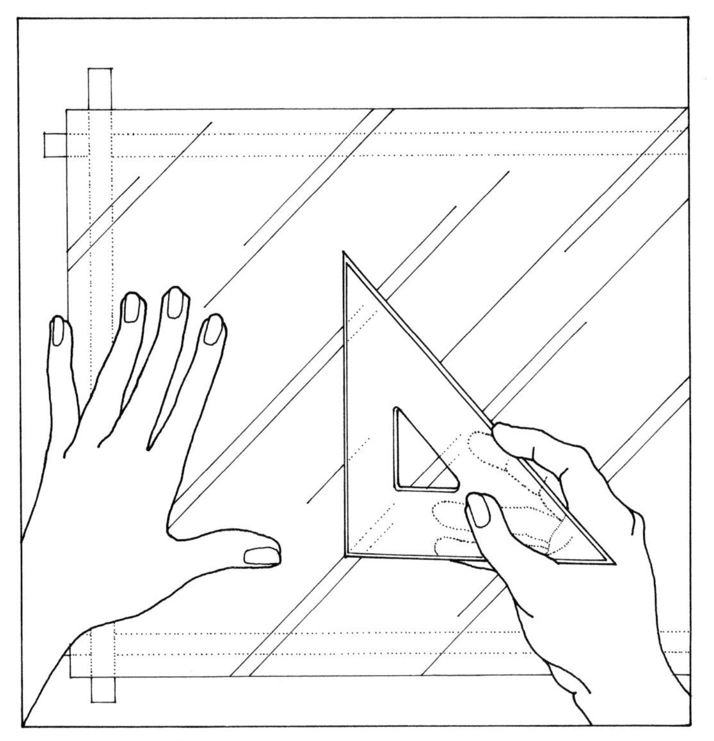

4.4 Burnishing frisket film

a single operation and avoid replacing masks.

If you decide to adopt the frisket-replacement strategy, the removed frisket should be stored flat on the slick side of a spare sheet of backing until it is reused. Also, allow a few minutes for the paint to dry before you replace the frisket. Failure to follow this precaution will ruin the illustration, because frisket film replaced over slightly moist airbrushing will later pluck away the paint surface when all the frisket pieces are finally removed.

To avoid the chance of paint creeping under the edge of a frisket, make a habit of burnishing the mask at regular intervals during the airbrushing stages, especially with more complex illustrations. This ensures that smaller pieces of remaining frisket do not get blown away by the airbrush jetstream. You can also cover the artwork with a frisket sheet backing and firmly run the edge of a ruler or triangle across the surface (fig. 4.4).

DRAFTING TAPE

Several different types of adhesive material can be used for masking small areas, such as drafting tape, certain types of clear plastic tape, and even sticky-backed labels, but they can only be used on more rugged boards and heavyweight watercolor papers. We recommend 3M drafting tape, especially for beginners, as it has less tack than its counterparts and is therefore much safer to use.

Always check adhesive materials (or any type of supplemental mask other than frisket film, for that matter) on a spot away from the artwork to see if it deposits any residue that will interfere with the spraytone.

LIQUID MASKS

Rubber-based masking fluid can also be painted onto the artwork surface to mask off small areas. This fluid forms a thin coat of latex that can be rubbed away with your finger or a soft eraser after spraying. Masking fluid is especially useful for intricate patterns or for creating textural effects with a paintbrush (see pages 18 and 91).

The traditional liquid mask is rubber cement, but we recommend Winsor & Newton's masking fluid because it has a yellow tint (whereas rubber cement is colorless), making it more visible and thus easier to apply and remove.

HAND-HELD MASKS

A multitude of hand-held masks can be improvised to create different types of edges and textural effects and also to control areas to be sprayed. These are mainly used as masks within masks—that is, in conjunction with frisket film when an exposed area requires supplementary color treatment. Such masks can be utilized from any found material, such as pieces of board or cardstock, pieces of string, cotton, wool, feathers, or any material that will stencil a desired effect.

Airbrush illustrators also frequently use paper masks. These masks can be cut or torn into the required shape and held at different distances and inclinations to produce varying contour effects. Hand-cut board or cardstock masks are recommended over the myriad different-shaped plastic hand-held masks available on the market. Plastic masks do not absorb overspray and, if reused when wet, can cause unwanted blemishes on the illustration.

Two popular hand-held masks are the teardrop mask and the L-shaped mask. The teardrop mask (fig. 4.5) is cut from cardstock and is about 4–5 in (10–13 cm) in length. It functions simply as a french curve for the masking of rounded or sinuous edges, such as shadows. Providing sweeping contours, it allows for great flexibility, creating hard-edged washes when held close to the surface and softer-edged washes when held slightly above the surface.

A pair of L-shaped masks (fig. 4.6)

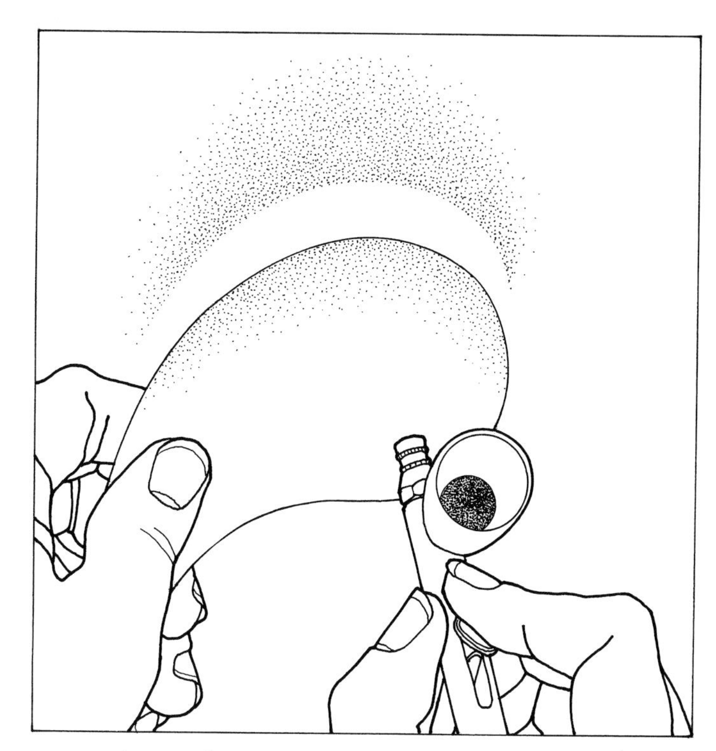

4.5 Teardrop mask

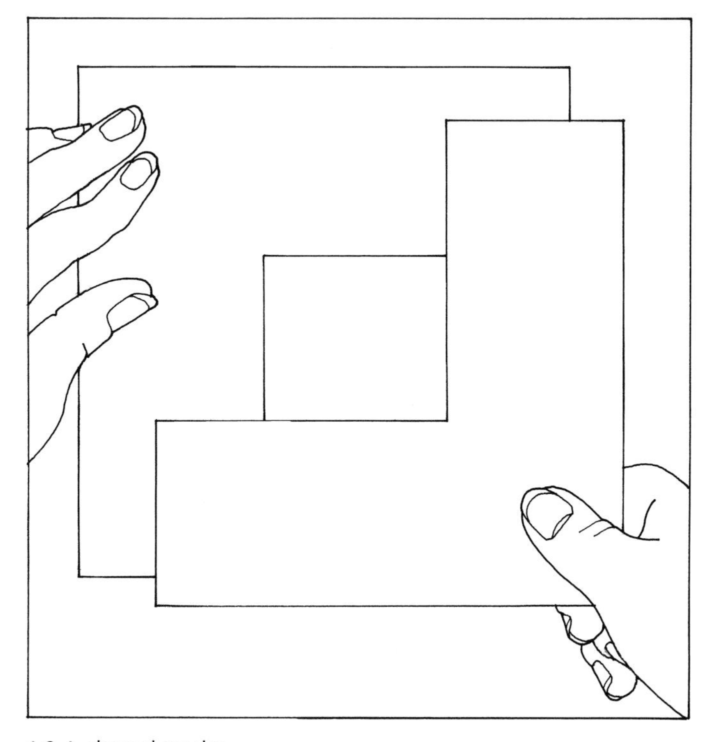

4.6 L-shaped masks

also provides a range of masking possibilities. Each arm should be approximately 1½ in (9 cm) wide and 5 in (13 cm) long along the longest side. Used individually they can mask short, straight edges and small right angles; in unison they can be used to mask rectangles, squares, and other cubic shapes.

EXERCISE 1 **Found Masks**

Divide a sheet of 22 x 30 in (56 x 76 cm) illustration board into twelve equal rectangles. Then collect a range of material to block or filter the spray, creating different textures, patterns, or shapes. Your collection can include cotton, wool, gravel, dried leaves, extruded plastic or metal screens, string of different thickness, perforated papers, etc.

Experiment on the board by holding or placing each material within the various rectangles. Spray around or through each mask to create a shape or an effect (fig. 4.7). Watch for marks that could be incorporated into future illustrations. For example, balls of cotton or wool can be used to simulate cumulus cloud formations; dry or decomposed leaves and small-scale vegetation such as lichen can be used to stencil trees, undergrowth, and foliage; and extruded plastic screens are excellent for airbrushing glass blocks in architectural elevations and perspectives. Work across the grid of effects using three different tonal values, and don't be afraid of superimposing a texture or pattern in one value over that of another value.

Opposite:
4.7 Student exercise: Effects using different experimental templates

SURFACE-PAINT INTERACTION

The relationship between the nature of the surface and the paint is an important one. As mentioned earlier, the characteristics of the surface affect the quality and appearance of the airbrushed image. The following exercise will allow you to develop a degree of familiarity with different types of surfaces.

EXERCISE 2
Surface-Pigment-Mask Effects

First, collect a wide range of different types of potential surfaces, including illustration board, watercolor paper (heavyweight and lightweight grades), yellow tracing paper, bond paper, Mylar, museum board, and colored papers such as charcoal and pastel papers. Then, using a pencil against a straightedge, divide a 22 x 30 in (56 x 76 cm) sheet of foamcore board into twelve equal squares. Trim each sample surface into a 7¼ in (18 cm) square and attach each to one square of the grid with adhesive spray mount. Write the name of the surface below each sample.

Load the airbrush with black paint and spray a series of lines across the face of each of the papers (fig. 4.8). This will demonstrate how different types of surfaces react to the spray application. The most obvious difference is that the thinner papers tend to buckle when wet. Also, different samples will have different drying times—harder, less absorbent surfaces, such as the slick and matte sides of Mylar, take much longer to dry and are more susceptible to curtaining (paint running down the surface). The

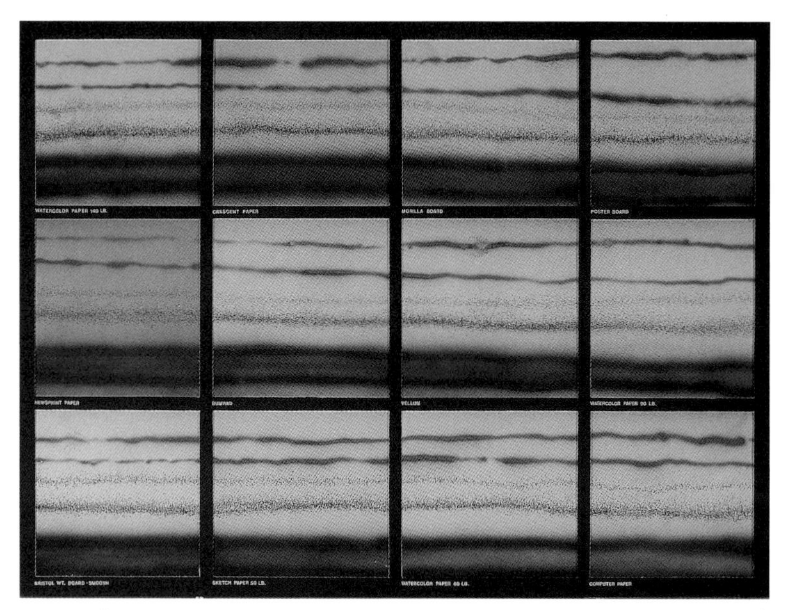

4.8 Surface test.

FIRST ROW: 1. Watercolor paper 140 lb. 2. Crescent paper 3. Morilla Board 4. Poster Board

SECOND ROW: 1. Newsprint paper 2. Bumwad 3. Vellum 4. Watercolor paper 90 lb.

THIRD ROW: 1. Bristol wt. board smooth 2. Sketch paper 50 lb. 3. Watercolor paper 50 lb. 4. Computer paper

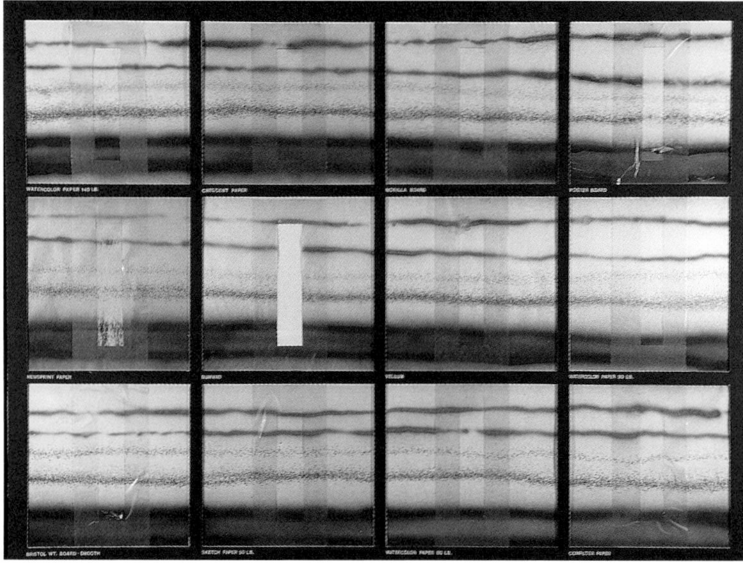

4.9 Aftereffects on different surfaces of frisket removal

absorbency of the surface also affects the visual quality of the paint—softer papers allow paint to sink in and thus appear slightly darker in value than less absorbent surfaces.

Next, cut three 3 in (8 cm) wide strips of frisket film and attach each across the center of each of the rows of paper samples. Use your knife to cut a small rectangular window at the center of each frisketed sample (remember to apply little or no pressure). Carefully lift one corner of the window with the point of the blade, and remove each window, noting the resulting effect (fig. 4.9).

This experiment has several advantages. First, it reveals something about the lightness of touch required when cutting frisket film, especially on thinner papers. Second, it shows how the tack of the frisket film behaves on the various samples. For instance, on softer papers, such as foamcore, tracing paper, and pastel paper, the frisket film breaks down the integrity of the surface by pulling up fibers. The more robust acetate, watercolor paper, and illustration board withstand abuse from the knife blade and release the frisket without surface damage. As mentioned earlier, rough watercolor papers are the most durable and easy to work on because they withstand frisket film, drafting tape, and Scotch tape. Cold-pressed papers and boards can also be used but do not readily accept Scotch tape. The smoother hot-pressed papers and boards have a much more delicate surface; when frisket film placed over sprayed areas is removed, some of the paint will be plucked away.

5 Getting Started: The Basic Building Blocks

All students of airbrush should undertake the four introductory exercises described in this chapter. Each illustrates one way, but not the only way, to achieve professional results. They also establish important tips, issues, and processes concerning airbrush technique.

These exercises not only provide a springboard for your first airbrush illustrations but also introduce you to the building blocks of form—the cube, cylinder, and sphere—as they look under a fixed source of light. Most of the objects in our visual environment derive from the geometry of these basic forms, their surfaces being made up of flat planes and rounded surfaces. Understanding how the airbrush can simulate the behavior of light, shade, and shadow on the surfaces of these forms will enable you to achieve convincing results. For instance, you will learn how light reflected back from adjacent surfaces causes the amount of shade or shadow on each plane to vary, creating a gradated tone. It is this interplay of light, shade, and shadow—and reflected light within shade and shadow—that defines the nature of planes and creates the illusion of form and space.

All of the following exercises use a single mask. Each exercise should be worked on a clean piece of Crescent board No. 110 trimmed to 12 x 10 in (30 x 25 cm).

Exercise 1 **Cube**

Start with an outline drawing of a cube shown as a simple perspective projection. Lightly but firmly draw it with a 4H pencil against a straightedge and add a shadow cast from a light source at the left (fig. 5.1). Make sure that the drawing is clean, unblemished, and free from the scars of excessive erasure, because any unwanted marks left under the spray will be difficult to remove. Then, completely cover the drawing with frisket film. Use an X-Acto blade against a metal straightedge to trace-cut

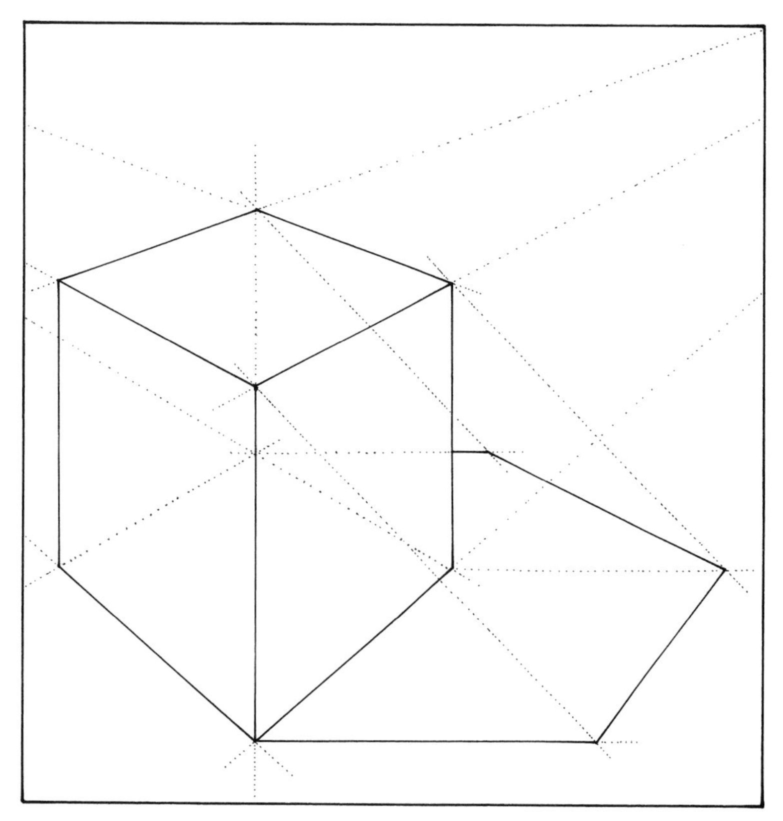

5.1 Outline drawing of a cube

the frisket along each line. Remember to use the gentlest of pressure when cutting the film.

The first area to be exposed for spraying—the shape of the projected shadow—will be the darkest. To remove this frisket, place the tip of the knife blade under one corner, lift the frisket, and, holding with the thumb, slowly remove the mask (fig. 5.2). Load the airbrush color cup with black. The shadow will ultimately be the darkest value in the image because it will be subjected to several passes. Thus, it is not necessary at this stage to achieve the final depth of value in the shadow. Always begin and end the airbrush pass just outside the exposed area, the initial spray allowing for a quick check on its efficacy immediately before bringing it into direct contact with the exposed area (fig. 5.3).

Now remove the frisket on the right-hand, shaded face of the cube. Spray the

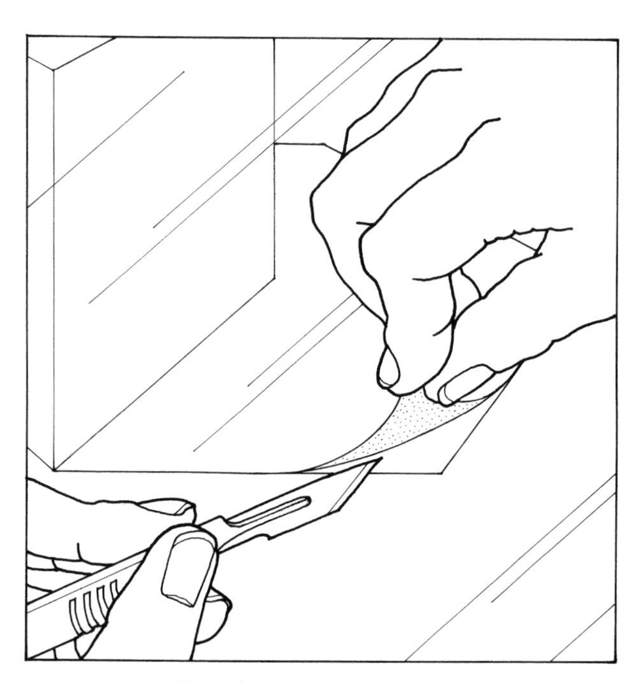

5.2 Removing the frisket

5.3 Establishing the shadow value

exposed area (the shaded face of the cube and the shadow) in diagonal passes from the upper left-hand corner to the bottom right-hand corner. Build up the tone in a series of layered passes with greater intensity in the upper left-hand area of the face, lightening the value as you move toward the lower, right-hand edge of the plane (fig. 5.4).

After the paint is dry, remove the mask from the left-hand cube face. Again, make a series of diagonal passes, allowing the darkest value to reside in the lower, outer left-hand area of the face. Continue diagonal passes to slowly build up the tone, allowing it to fade in intensity as it nears the top corner (fig. 5.5). As each face of the cube is successively revealed and remains exposed, the airbrushing of each plane in turn allows overspray to progressively and subtly build up the tone of the previously established planes.

Now remove the mask from the top face of the cube and apply a light value tone using horizontal passes. The uppermost (far) corner of this face should have the greatest intensity of tone, with the tone quickly fading as it descends into the lower (near) corner (fig. 5.6). After the paint is dry, carefully remove the remaining mask from the surrounding surface to reveal the finished result (fig. 5.7).

What have you achieved? With only a single mask, a rather powerful visual illusion of a cube bathed in bright sunlight has been created—its glowing effect resulting from the value modulation on each of its faces. Note that the cube responds to two conditions of light: direct light and reflected light. Reflected light is a phenomenon that appears in shaded and shadowed

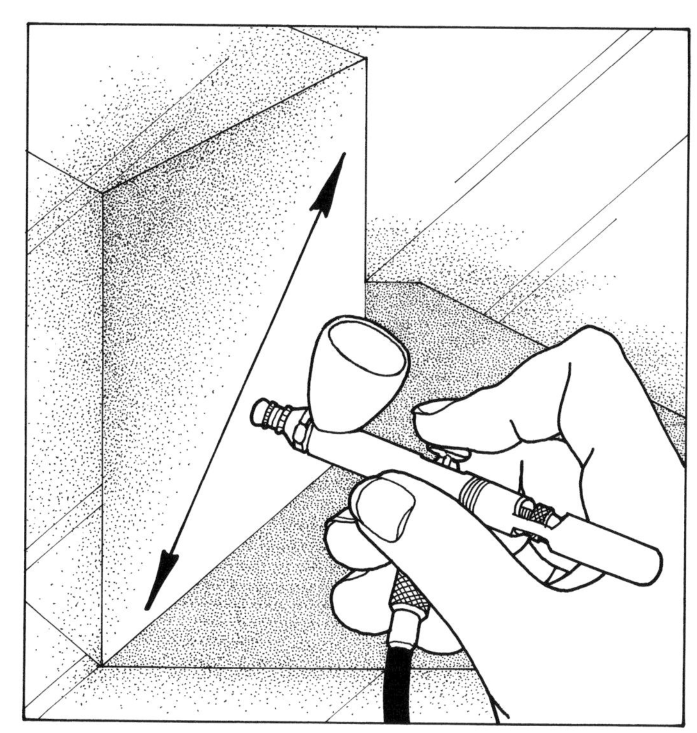

5.4 Building up the shaded plane

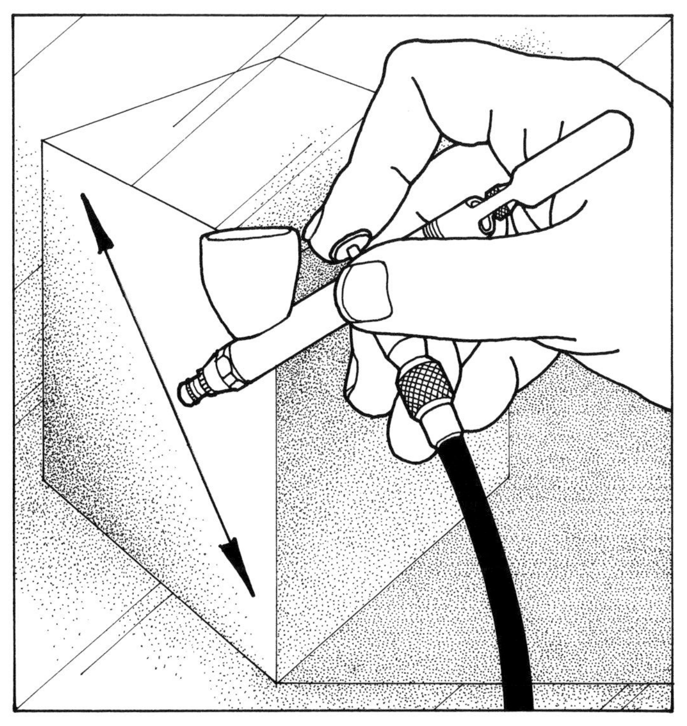

5.5 Airbrushing the lefthand plane

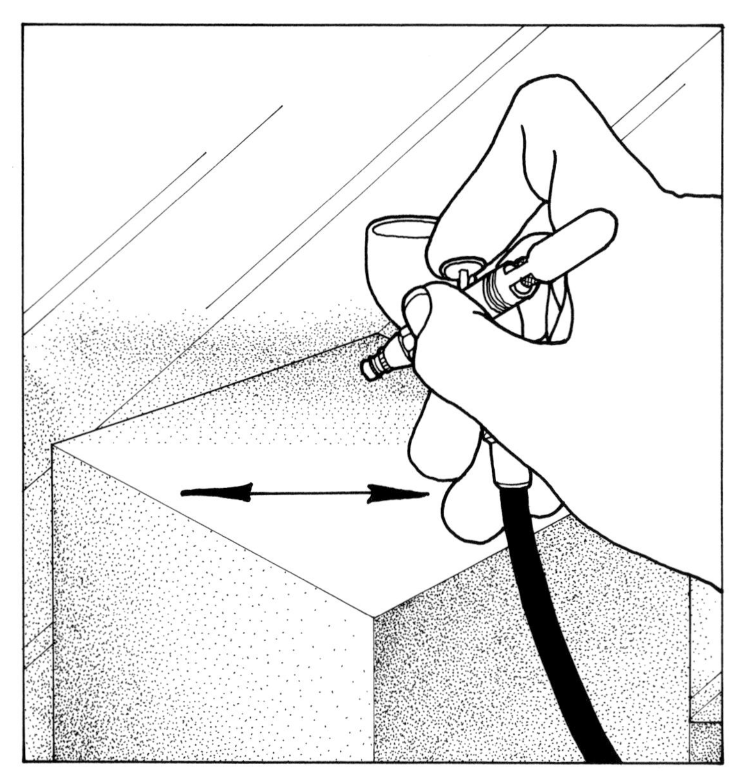
5.6 Airbrushing the light-receiving plane

5.7 The completed airbrushed cube

planes. It is caused when a certain amount of direct light is deflected from sunlit planes into areas of shade and shadow. This scattering of light induces value to lighten within the body of the shade or shadow and causes their tones to appear to flicker and fluctuate. It is a subtle effect simulated in drawings by many architects (see, for example, the pencil drawings of Cesar Pelli). However, by slightly emphasizing value at the nearer corners of the right-hand face of the cube, the further edges of the left-hand face, and the further edge of the top face, the incidence of reflected light comes into play. It is a recognition of the incidence of reflected light that, also causing a heightened contrast in the structure of value, acts to intensify the illusion of three dimensions. More than any other medium, the airbrush can effortlessly recreate this effect.

This exercise also illustrates that, generally speaking, airbrushing is a technique that sprays from dark to light. Different degrees of value are achieved not as a result of different paint consistencies, but of the progressive buildup of spraytones—the successive spraying of each exposed area. A common mistake made by beginners is to overairbrush the darker and mid-value areas (i.e., the shadow and shaded plane) in the first pass, resulting in a rather dark and tonally ill-defined illustration.

Sometimes judging the value of an area being airbrushed is difficult. This especially tends to happen when airbrushing darker values and when the exposed area to be sprayed is surrounded by oversprayed frisket or is otherwise isolated from adjacent or similar values already established elsewhere in the illustration, making any direct visual comparison difficult. There are two methods of avoiding this problem. One is to regularly compare the value buildup of a spraytone against a small piece of white board. This is a technique used by many artists and illustrators who quickly compare a value with the white of a piece of board held against a tone or color in order to visually judge its degree of departure from white. When a more critical judgment is called for, you can utilize a value chart similar to that illustrated in figure 3.11. As each step in the chart corresponds to a specific number of passes, an estimation of the required passes to achieve a value can be calculated. For an even more precise check, the selected tone on the value chart can, at intervals, be placed directly alongside the spraytone buildup until a perfect value match is achieved.

The rendition of a basic cube in figure 5.7 can, abstractly, represent a sunlit architectural form. Many of the seemingly complex architectural illustrations shown in the following chapters are merely variations of, and elaborations on, this simple exercise.

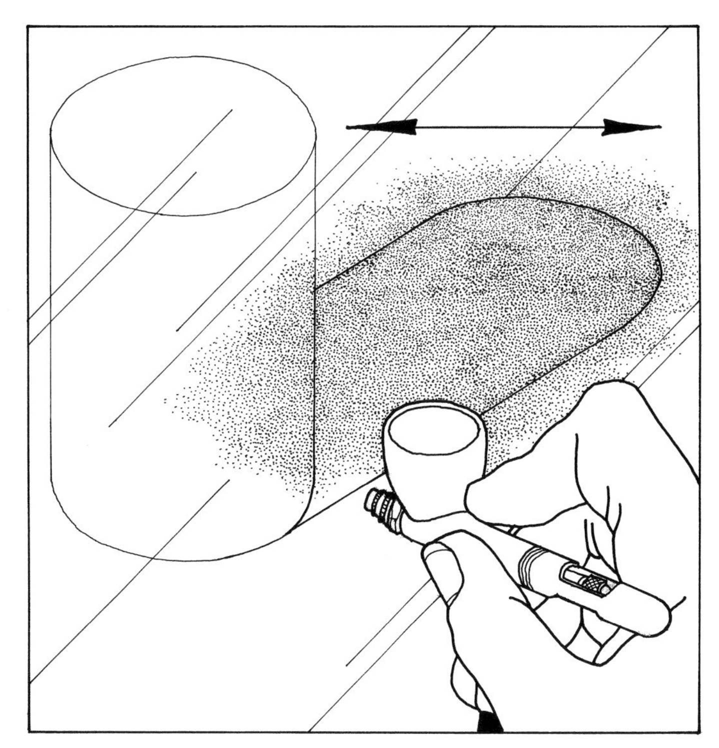

5.8 Airbrushing the shadow

Exercise 2 **Cylinder**

Draw the outline of a cylinder and its shadow in pencil on illustration board, protect it with a frisket, and cut the frisket as you did in the first exercise. Remove the frisket covering the cast shadow and, using horizontal passes with the airbrush, establish a preliminary dark value (fig. 5.8). Again, it is not necessary to achieve the full weight of value at this stage.

Next, remove the mask protecting the drum of the cylinder. This mask will be

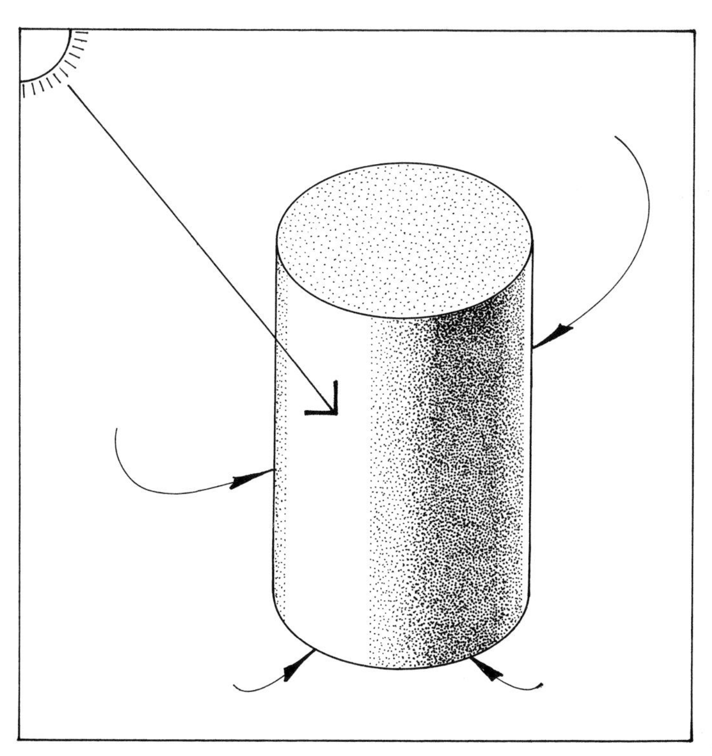

5.9 Conceptual guide

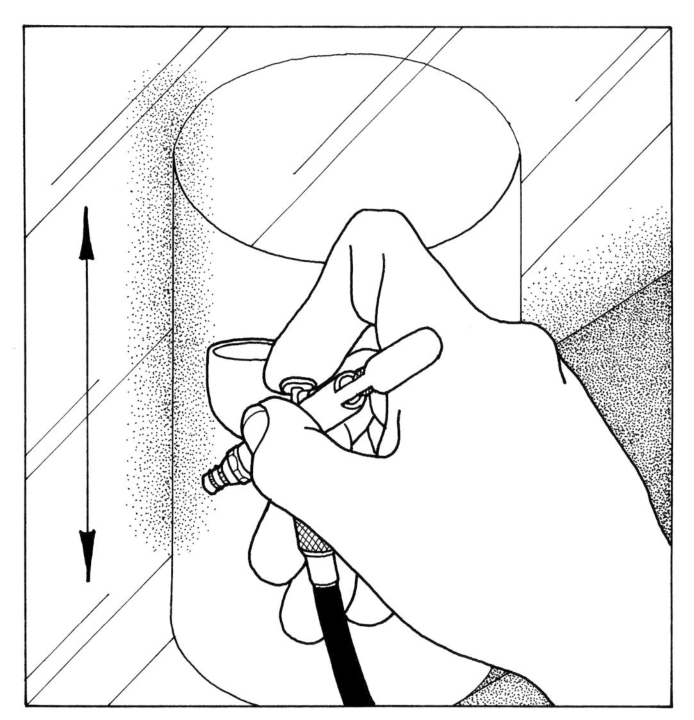
5.10 The initial pass

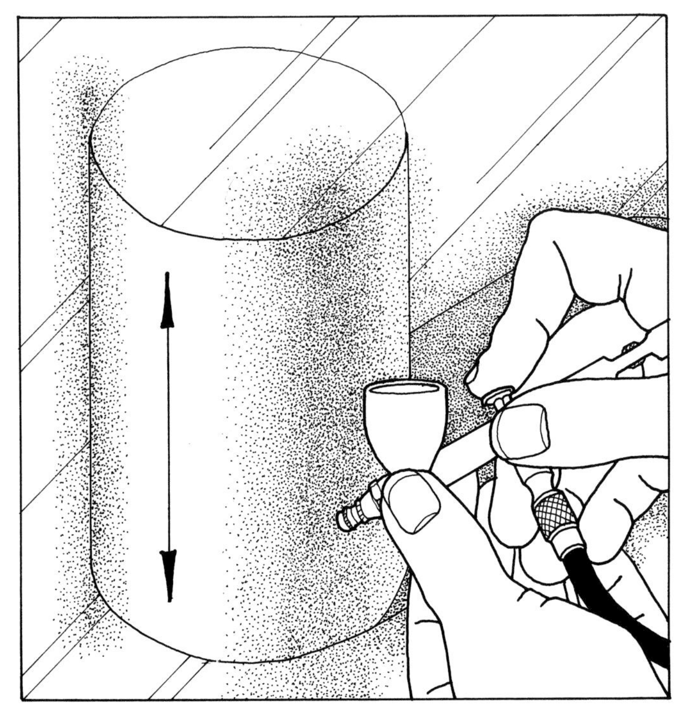
5.11 Modeling the band of shade on the drum

reused later, so carefully store it by gently attaching it to the face of a spare frisket sheet backing. Two important elements of the visual experience of the cylinder are its highlight and its band of reflected light. Keep a mental diagram of their incidence on the drum in mind when rendering its illusion (fig. 5.9). Continue by airbrushing its left-hand side. Spray this in a soft value, keeping passes parallel to the edge of the drum (fig. 5.10). Follow this with a soft spraytone on the right of the cylinder that fades toward the right-hand edge and at a point just right of the center of the drum. This preliminary value establishes the band of highlight and also the narrower strip of reflected light along the outer right edge of the cylinder. While taking care to keep parallel to the vertical edge of the drum, complete final passes to achieve the appearance of a seamless fade, building up the body of the shade and increasing its value at the center of its band (fig. 5.11).

Now, carefully replace the mask from the cylinder drum so that it is relocated precisely in its original position (fig. 5.12). Should replacement prove difficult, or if the frisket is damaged, simply remask the immediate area with a new piece of frisket and recut.

Once the mask is replaced, remove the frisket protecting the top of the cylinder and spray lightly, using horizontal passes to emphasize a slightly darker edge at the upper (far) edge of the plane (fig. 5.13). Finally, remove all remaining frisket to reveal the completed airbrushed cylinder (fig. 5.14).

This exercise illustrates the way light behaves on cylindrical and curving surfaces. This visual effect can be enhanced by introducing the subtle incidence of

5.12 Replacing the frisket

5.13 Spraying the top

5.14 The completed airbrushed cylinder

shimmering light into both shaded and shadowed areas. This should begin to inform the way you look at the visual world—that is, you should become more aware of how light and reflected light affect the appearance of basic forms. Such visual phenomena play a role in the way we render architectural form; it is a visual effect fully exploited in the illustrations featured on pages 67, 98, and 100.

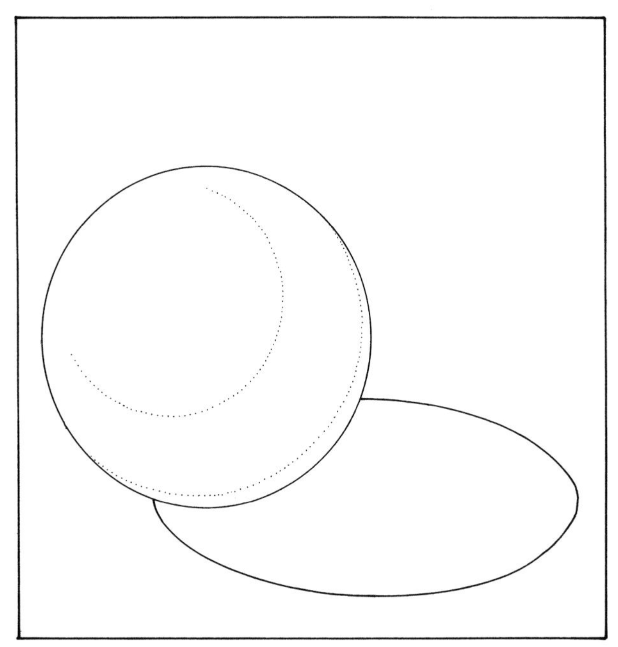

5.15 Outline drawing of a sphere

Exercise 3. **Sphere**

Although the airbrushing of a sphere appears straightforward, it can prove the most difficult of these initial exercises. This is because there are no internal edges to mask; the impression of form must be built up using freehand spraying alone. This requires good finger control and involves moving the whole arm—not just the wrist—to depict the flowing, regular curves of the sphere.

Using a compass, draw a circle approximately 4 in (10 cm) in diameter, and add a cast shadow (fig. 5.15). Place the frisket film over the form and trace-cut it and its shadow freehand with the X-Acto knife. Remove the mask from the shadow, and begin airbrushing with several passes over the exposed area (fig. 5.16).

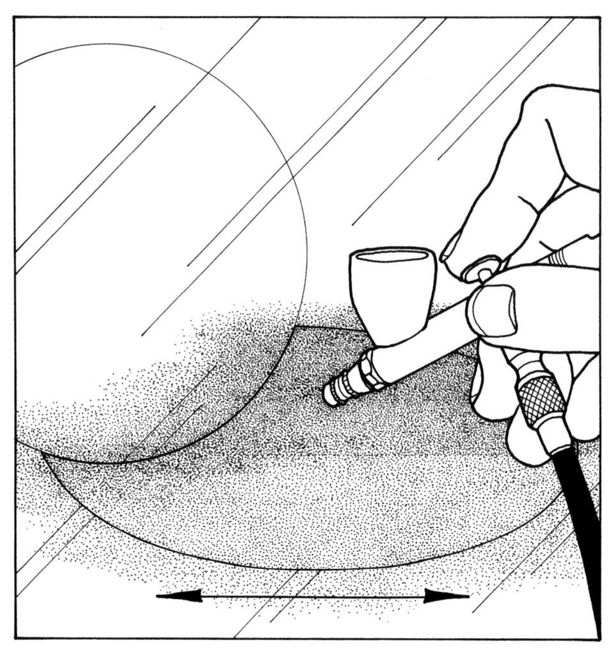

5.16 Establishing the shadow

Next, remove the frisket protecting the circle and, working close to the surface of the illustration (and remembering to begin each pass outside of the exposed area), gradually build up a light ring of shade completely around the edge of the circle. Use steady, circular sweeps.

The illusion of three dimensions will

result from the crescent-shaped curves of the darker shade fading toward the center of the sphere (fig. 5.17). Reflected light plays an important role here, too—in this case as a small crescent of subdued light along the underside of the sphere.

The sphere is complete after a buildup of shade has been airbrushed in circular passes around the outer edge of the sphere. Remove the surrounding frisket to expose the completed illustration (fig. 5.18).

The success of this exercise relies upon a clear understanding of how light and shade appear to model the spherical form. This particular exercise may take more than one attempt; keep trying until your rendition comes close to the one shown.

5.17 Modeling the curve of the shade

5.18 The completed airbrushed sphere

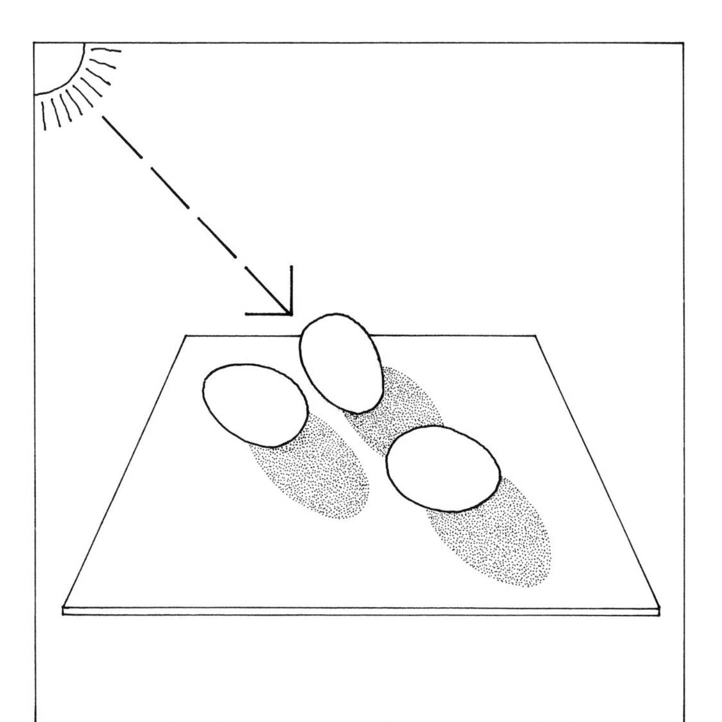

5.19 Still life with eggs

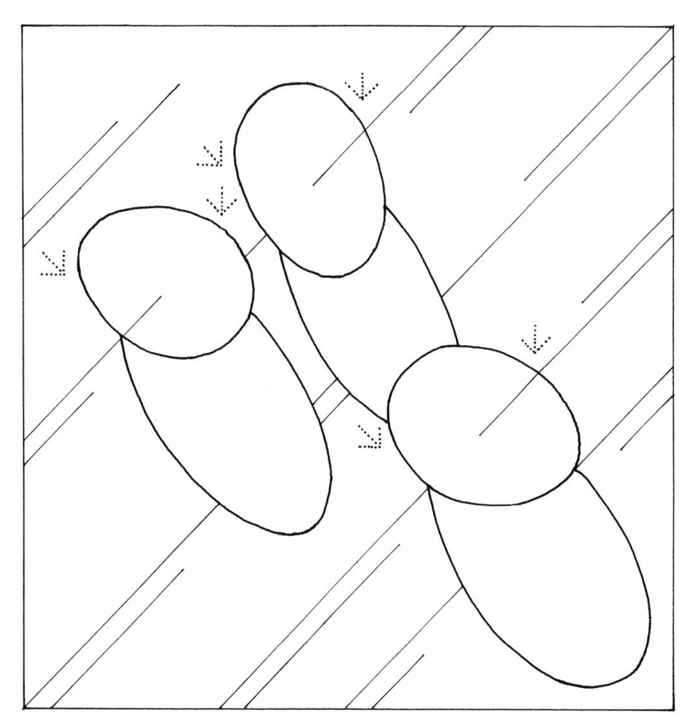

5.20 Guide arrows

Exercise 4. **Eggs**

This exercise reinforces the experience of freehand airbrushing of rounded surfaces. Arrange two or three white eggs in an asymmetrical still life group on a sheet of white card so that each egg and its shadow remains separate. The still life should be lit by a diagonal overhead light source—that is, placed in strong sunlight or under a spotlight (fig. 5.19).

This exercise requires accuracy of drawing with keen observation of the behavior of light. Therefore, it is important to spend a few minutes studying the structure and shape of the highlights, shades, and shadows—as well as the incidental areas of reflected light—as they appear on the forms. In order to ascertain value relationships in a still life, many artists squint as they observe the values. This eliminates extraneous details and allows for a more analytical, exclusive assessment of the value structure.

The drawing should be an accurate outline of the cluster of eggs and their shadows. After applying and trace-cutting the frisket, carefully remove the masks protecting the shadows and establish their dark value, being careful to use the airbrush to render any incidence of reflected light.

The eggs can then be exposed in turn or, as with the student illustration (see fig. 5.21), simultaneously exposed and airbrushed in one freehand spraying operation. To guide the arc of shade, draw two guide arrows in pencil just outside the contour of each egg. These arrows should indicate the starting point and direction of the curve of shade and will help guide the beginning

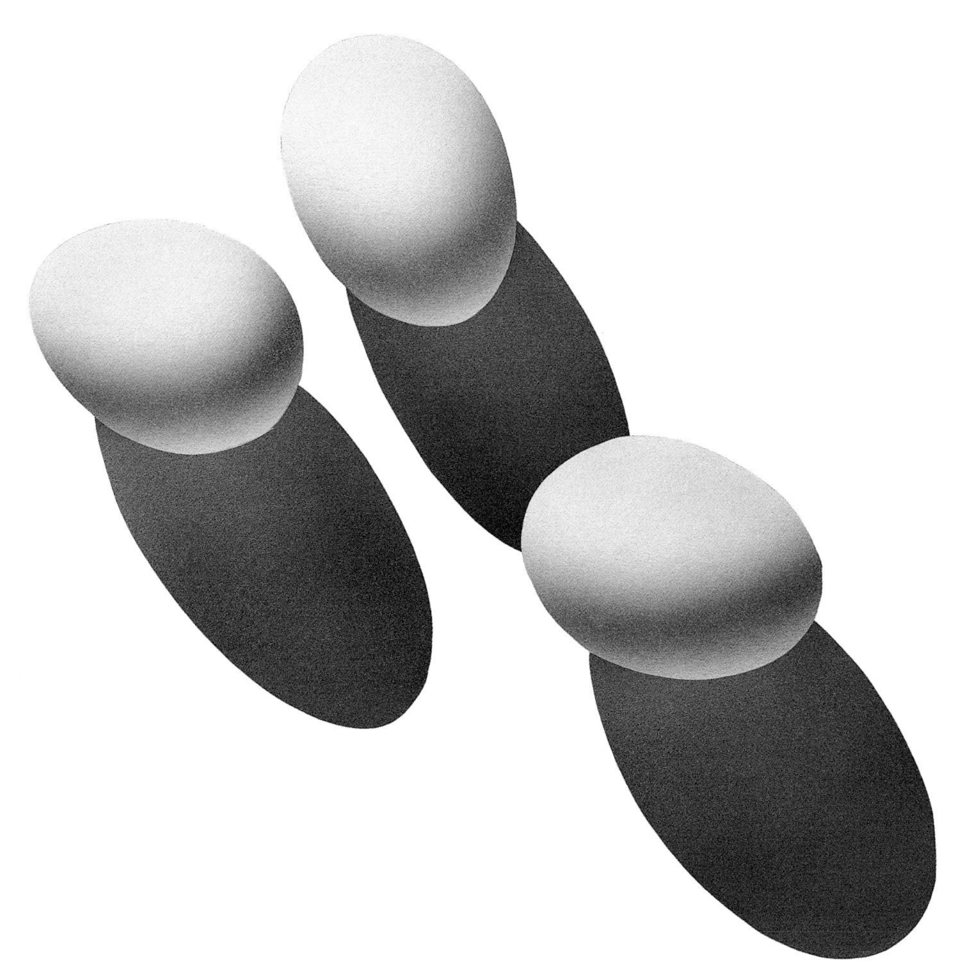

5.21 Student exercise: The completed airbrushed egg shapes

and end of each sweep of the airbrush (fig. 5.20).

As in the sphere exercise, begin airbrushing by establishing a light halo of tone around the outer edge of the egg. Then, using the guide arrows to direct the next sequence of passes, build up the darker value on the curve of shade. The dark value should quickly fade both upward into the highlight and downward into the region of reflected light.

Airbrushing the egg shapes takes little time; the success of this illustration relies upon accuracy of airbrushing and the gradated density of the curving area of shade (fig. 5.21).

These four exercises should help you gain further experience in airbrush control and develop confidence in its use as a rendering tool. Therefore, before moving to the next stage, revisit the exercises for which you did not achieve results similar to the student examples shown.

6 Image-Building: One and Two Friskets

The next step is to apply basic airbrush principles to a series of illustrations. These images represent the first excursion into more ambitious picture-making involving the use of one or two friskets. The exercises in this chapter will help you rehearse the all-important planning stage that should precede any application of spray. This is the stage when the development of an illustration is planned in a step-by-step sequence in order to provide a logical, convenient process—that is, one that economizes on the number of friskets.

Three introductory exercises worked in black and using one and two friskets are followed by a short exercise that studies the behavior of light. A concluding exercise involves the first color change. The drawings for these exercises may be done either freehand from direct observation or taken from a preexisting image. For your first airbrush illustration, choose a subject relatively uncomplicated in form and free from excessive detail. Forms with curves and corners and with smooth or reflective surfaces are excellent for airbrushing. These can be found around the home—for example, a piece of furniture, television set, toaster, or guitar. If you don't want to draw from direct observation, photograph the object of interest and process it as a 35 mm slide. You can also make photographs from source images found in magazines. Project the slide of the image onto a wall-mounted sheet of illustration board. The illustration board acts as the screen. Adjust the slide projection until you get the right size and location on the board. Working directly in the beam of the projected slide, make an outline drawing with a 4H pencil. Carefully trace the pattern of value or color constituting the structure of the image.

Whether you are working from direct observation or a photograph, the drawing stage should involve a delineated breakdown of the projected image into its component parts. In other words, you must see the object as an abstract pattern. Let's take a moment to clarify what this means.

Traditionally, drawing involves the delineation of shape—that is, tracing the form's silhouette. This is one aspect of the way we perceive, but it isn't the whole picture. For example, if we look closely at a scene, or a photograph of a scene, we can detect a pattern of discernible shapes caused by the incidence of differing contours of value and color. These shapes, or "perceptual patches," form the basic structural network of an image. Each shape in the network represents a specific value or color that, to a lesser or greater extent, differs from that of its neighbor. Indeed, it is this difference that allows us to discern the whole. In other words, if we closely scrutinize the source (or the source image), we find a fascinating and unpredictable structure of interlocking shapes. This structure is the very heart of the picture, for it is this arrangement of patches or shapes that allows the brain to read space and form. This essential pattern—that is, the one that governs spatial meaning in human perception—is demonstrated in figure 6.1.

6.1 Mapping an image

The incidence and intensity of this pattern of values and colors responds to the intensity and direction of the light source. This vital ingredient can be isolated by exclusively recording the precise shapes of only the shades and shadows (fig. 6.2). If we look at the basic delineation of shapes that define the constituent elements in the original view, we find that each has textural attributes that communicate a range of environmental surfaces (see the illustration on page 74 for an example of this).

6.2 Value structure of an image

A fundamental understanding of these perceptual patterns is important when you make a drawing in preparation for an airbrush rendering. The line you use must be rigorously clean and precise so as to provide an accurate guide during the frisket-cutting stage.

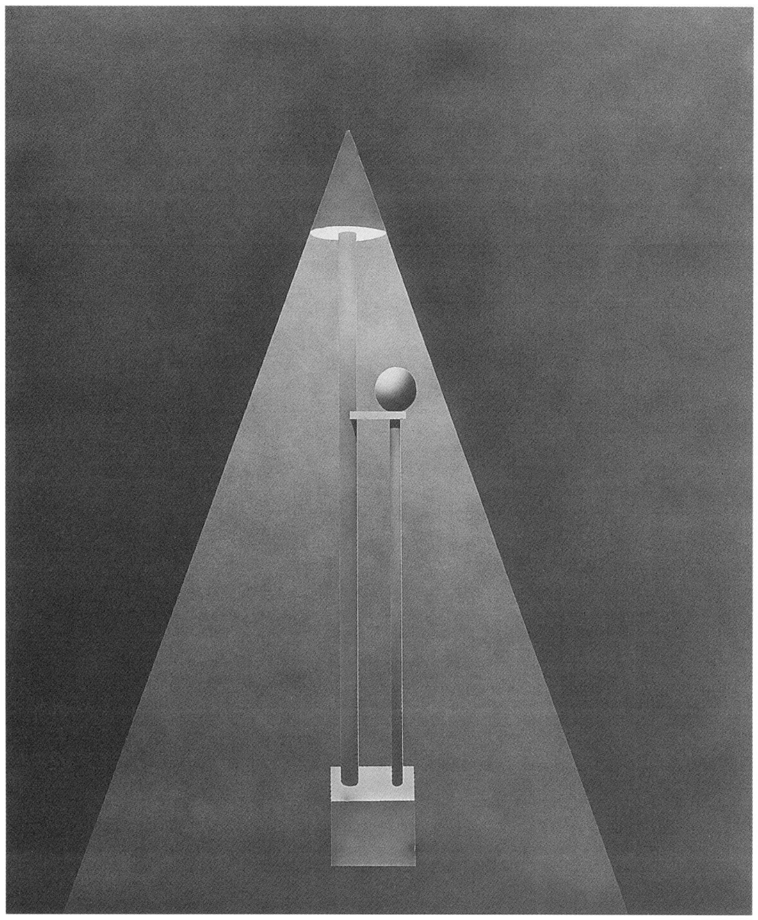

6-3 Lamp stand

Demonstration: **Lamp Stand**

Watercolor on illustration board,
20 x 30 in (51 x 76 cm)

Figures 6.3–6.9 illustrate one student's initial attempt at producing a complete airbrushed image of a lamp stand using a single frisket. It involves frisket cutting, removal, and replacement. Using your own drawing of a similar subject matter, you may wish to airbrush your first illustration using this demonstration as a guide. As the demonstration involves the airbrushing of a collection of basic geometric forms, together with the rendition of a variegated background spraytone, this and the following demonstrations will provide an excellent progression from the earlier exercises. Indeed, many of the basic airbrush principles and techniques, already established, will now be simply reapplied to the production of a more complete pictorial representation.

A 35 mm slide photographed from a found print of a lamp stand was projected onto a wall-mounted illustration board and traced with a 4H pencil with a straightedge, compass, and ellipse guide. When the drawing was finished, the board was placed flat and the drawing protected with frisket film. The border around the drawing was masked by scraps of plain paper. The line drawing was then completely trace-cut with an X-Acto knife and then placed on the easel for the airbrushing phase.

Next, the masks protecting the two small shadows cast at the top of the vertical columns and the mask protecting the sphere were removed; the latter was stored for reuse on a spare frisket sheet backing.

Using the original print as a guide,

6-4 Lamp stand airbrushing sequence: Step 1

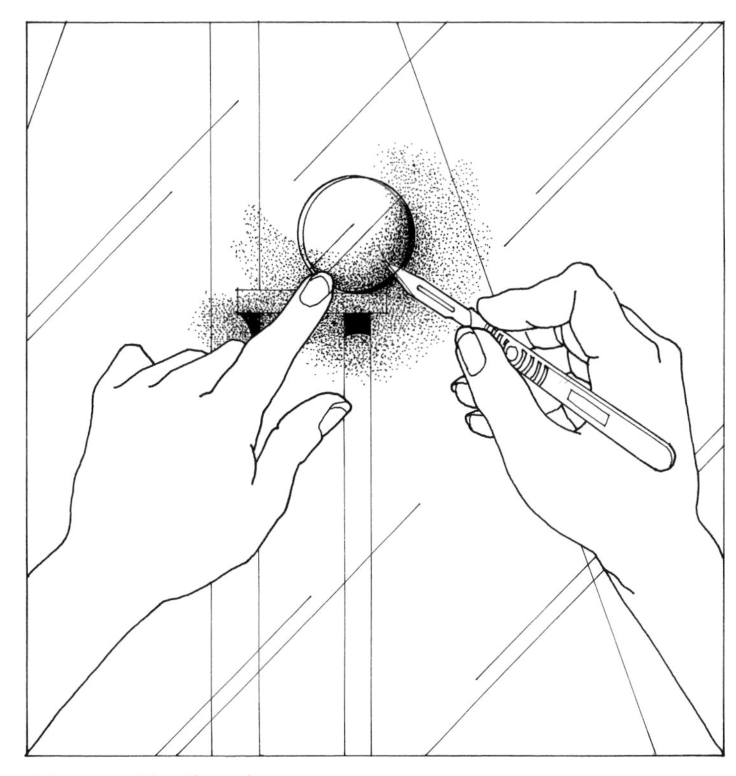

6-5 Remasking the sphere

the student airbrushed the sphere freehand as indicated on page 58 and added the dark tone of the two small shadows on the vertical supports (fig. 6.4). Because they would be unaffected by subsequent overspray, these small shadows were left exposed throughout the airbrushing sequence. To protect the highlight on the sphere, the student carefully replaced the stored mask (fig. 6.5).

The student continued the frisket removal, airbrushing, and mask replacement cycle for each of the basic geometric forms—the cube base, the cylindrical supports, and the conical lamp shade. The two visible faces of the cube were airbrushed in two steps: first, exposing the darker plane and building up its value before replacing the frisket; second, exposing the light plane and spraying a hint of tone before replacing the mask. Then the mask protecting the cone was removed, the area sprayed, and the frisket replaced (fig. 6.6).

Next, the two cylindrical supports were exposed and airbrushed (fig. 6.7). Again, their masks were carefully replaced.

At this point in the spraying sequence, most of the frisket remained intact. Two pieces on the lamp remained unsprayed—the ellipse at the base of cone and the horizontal bar below the sphere—as they were intended to appear as white paper in the final illustration.

To complete the illustration, the student removed the frisket protecting the darker background area surrounding

6-6 Lamp stand airbrushing sequence: Step 2

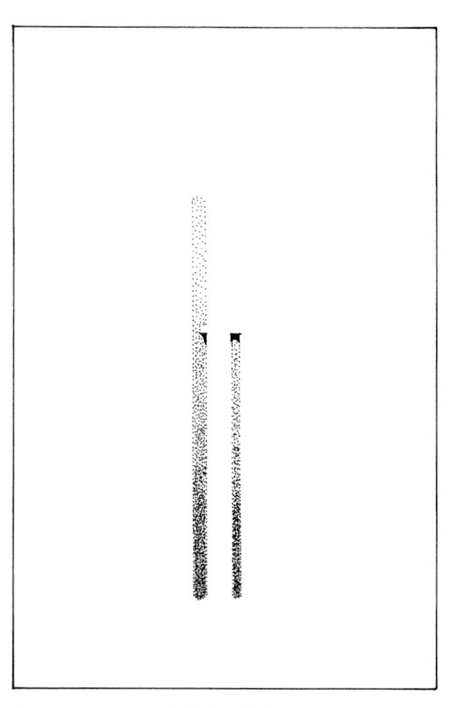

6-7 Lamp stand airbrushing sequence: Step 3

6-8 Lamp stand airbrushing sequence: Step 4

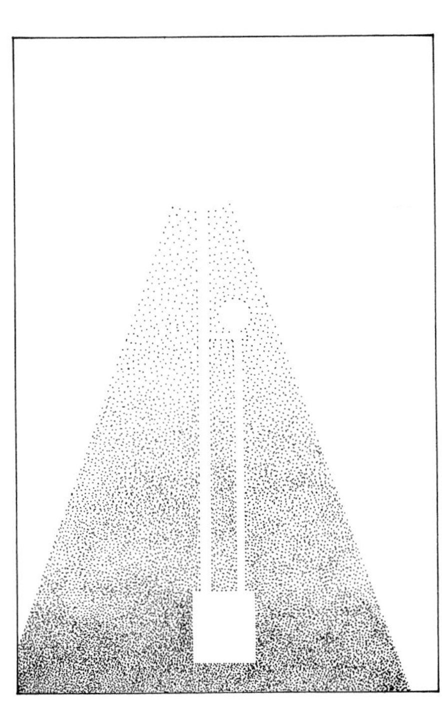

6-9 Lamp stand airbrushing sequence: Step 5

the beam of light and freely sprayed the area in broad sweeps to build up the depth of value (fig. 6.8). With the frisket on the lamp stand remaining in place, the student then removed the mask on the beam of light. The dark background was left exposed because it would be unaffected by the subtle wash on the beam of light (fig. 6.9).

The background value on this illustration is rather patchy and imperfect in nature. Fortunately, in this case, it is not detrimental to the overall atmospheric nature of the image. The ability to lay down a large, even area of spray comes with practice, often being achieved by an accumulation of horizontal passes overlaid with vertical passes (see page 38). Also apparent is the problem of frisket replacement, evidenced by the two glowing lines along the right-hand edges of the vertical cylindrical supports. The friskets' slight overlap onto the background area caused a mismatch that appeared as fine lines of white paper. Apart from ensuring that friskets are perfectly replaced before the next spraying stage, you can avoid this mistake by working out a cutting and spraying strategy that circumvents the need for frisket replacement. Most of the illustrations that follow are produced without frisket replacement.

The development of this illustration did not depend on the exact order of stages previously described. Apart from the fundamental rule of spraying dark values before light values, the airbrushing of the cube, cylinders, and sphere could have been carried out in any order. However, the spraying sequence should always be planned before airbrushing begins. We consider this in the next demonstration.

DEMONSTRATION: **Aalto Chair**

Watercolor on illustration board,
22 x 30 in (56 x 76 cm)

This illustration (fig. 6.10) began with a careful study of the original image to predetermine the sequence of ascending values and spraying stages. After the source image was visually "dismantled" according to its value structure, a reference drawing was made to indicate the sequence of airbrushing stages from dark to light (fig. 6.11).

Next, the student made a line drawing of the chair, covered it with frisket, and trace-cut the lines. As usual, the darkest regions of the image—inside the scroll at each end of the seat, the slits in the backrest, and the shadow cast on the floor—were exposed and sprayed first (fig. 6.12).

Then the dark, inside planes of the chair arms and the crossbar were revealed and sprayed (leaving exposed

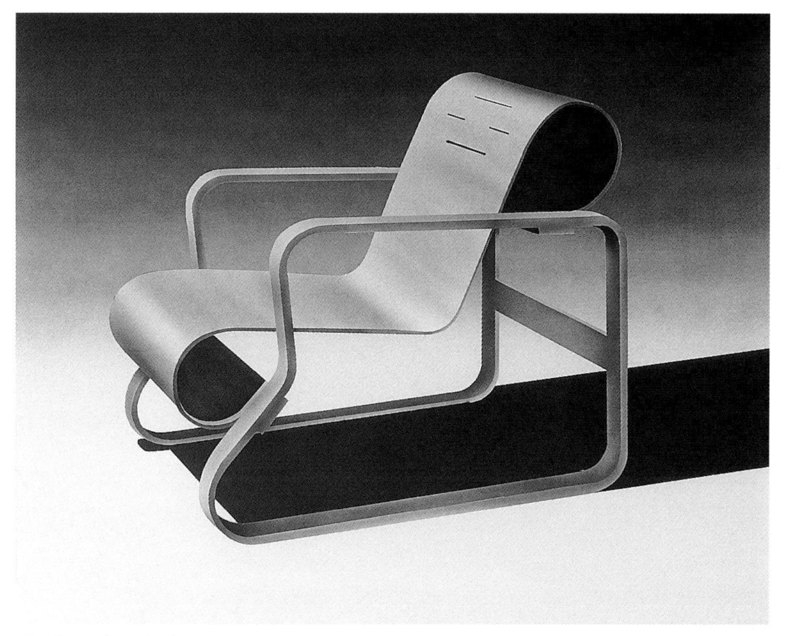

6-10 Aalto chair

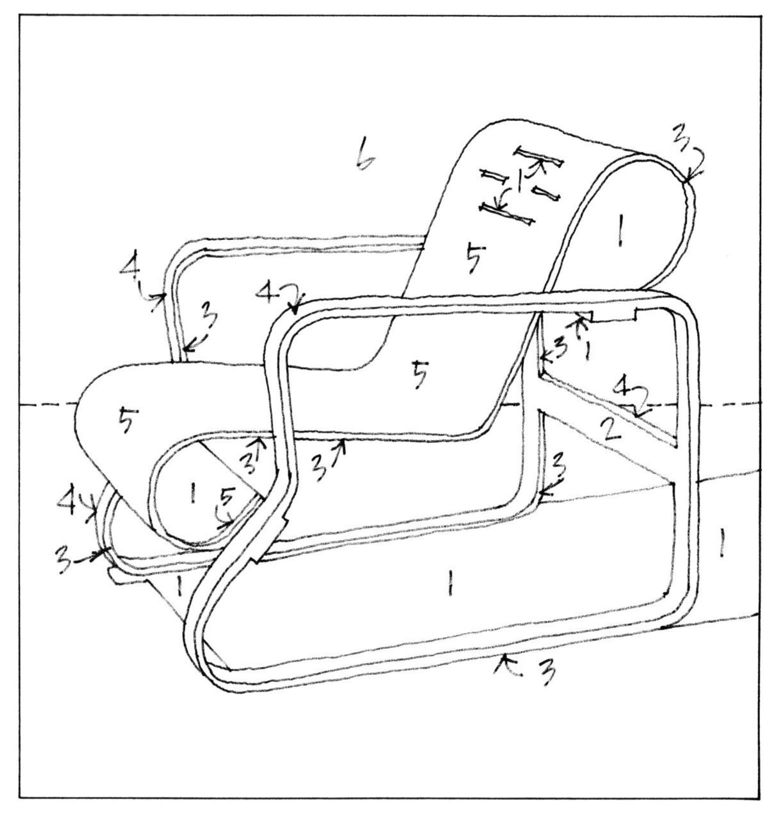

6-11 Reference drawing: Sequence of stages

the areas sprayed first). Additional passes were used to deepen the value at the point of their curves (fig. 6.13).

The set of planes with the next-lightest value—the vertical side plane of the arms and the edge of the seat—was then revealed and sprayed with a subtle variety of soft value passes (fig. 6.14). In order to recognize the slight shimmer in this tone—a subtle effect apparent in the source image—the vertical arm planes were airbrushed in a fluctuating value, overspray from this causing a similar effect on the exposed and slightly darker inside arm planes.

The penultimate value step was that of the tops of the arm rests. These friskets were removed and, to suggest highlights, lightly airbrushed to emphasize the value just below their curves (fig. 6.15).

The last stage in the rendition of the chair itself focused on the curving plane of the seat. This was lightly airbrushed with all the remaining elements of the chair exposed. Diagonal passes following the lateral direction of the chair

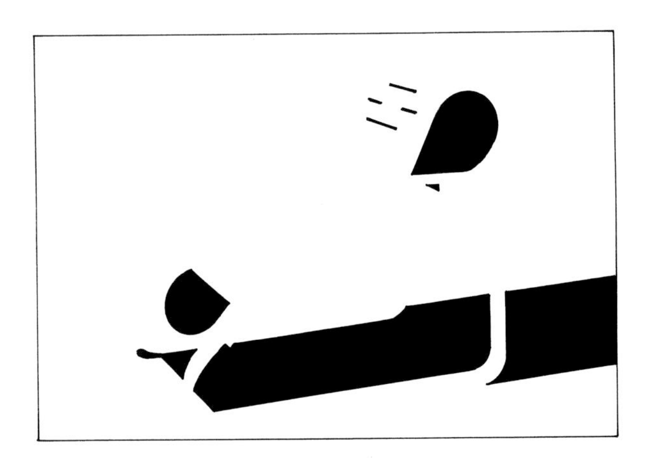

6.12 Chair airbrushing sequence: Step 1

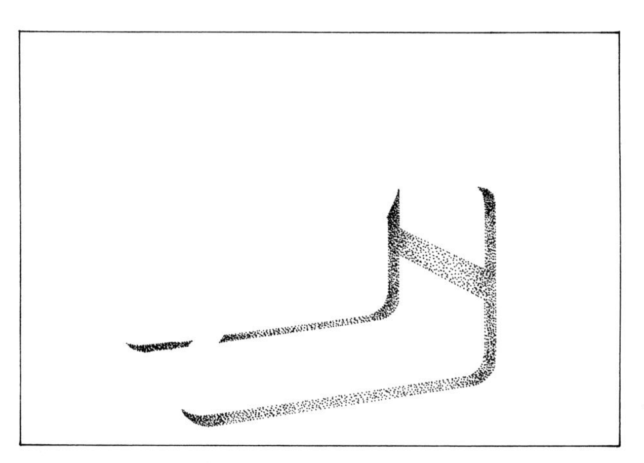

6.13 Chair airbrushing sequence: Step 2

plane were used in a manner similar to that demonstrated in the cylinder exercise in chapter 5. Light values were used around the curves to form highlights, and darker bands were added at the extreme ends of the scroll (fig. 6.16).

Finally, all the remaining frisket was removed and a new frisket applied. The new frisket was cut to protect the chair, and the mask around the chair was removed to expose the background. The background was then subjected to a gradated spraytone that faded downward from dark to light (fig. 6.17). This gradated spraytone resulted from a series of horizontal passes concentrated in the upper part of the area. Their accumulation produced a value that, even in its darkest region, was slightly lighter than the darkest shadows on the chair.

This visual breakdown of the values of the source image should occur every time you begin an illustration. It will help you not only determine the airbrush sequence, but also learn about how images are constructed.

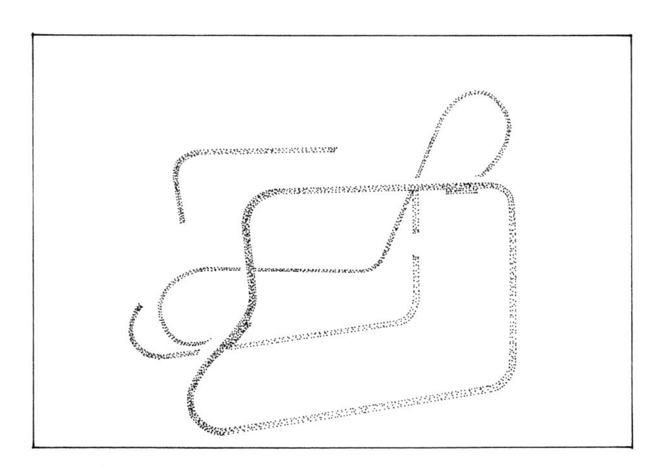

6.14 Chair airbrushing sequence: Step 3

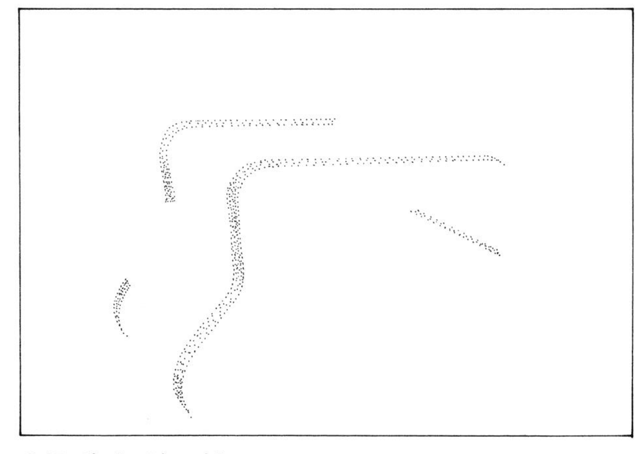

6.15 Chair airbrushing sequence: Step 4

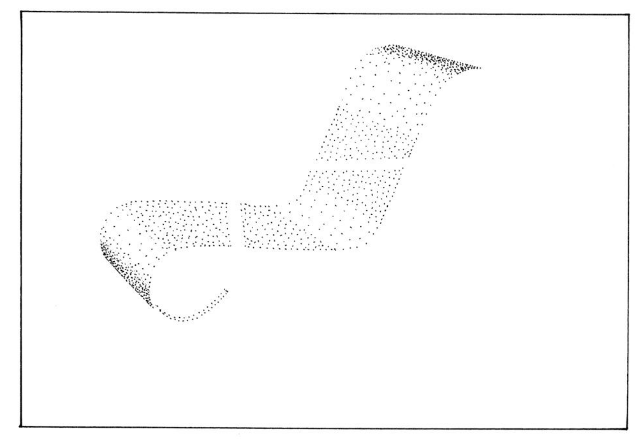

6.16 Chair airbrushing sequence: Step 5

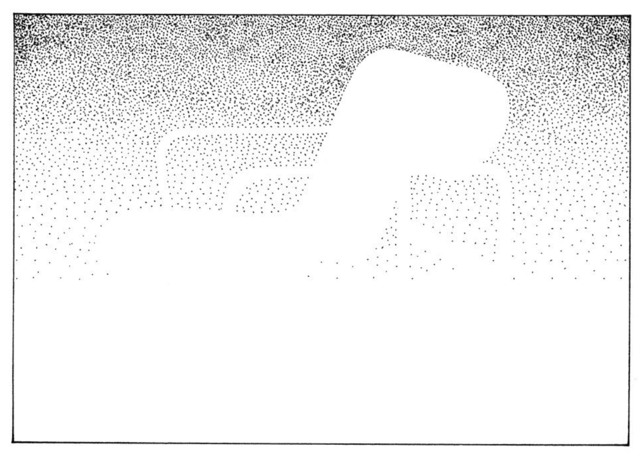

6.17 Chair airbrushing sequence: Step 6

6.18 Atrium ceiling at Richard Meier's High Museum, Atlanta

6.19 Atrium airbrushing sequence: Step 1

DEMONSTRATION:

Atrium Ceiling, Richard Meier's High Museum, Atlanta

Watercolor on illustration board,
22 x 30 in (56 x 76 cm)

At first glance, this rendering (fig. 6.18) appears to be a highly complex architectural illustration. However, derived from a 35 mm slide taken on a school trip to Atlanta, it is nothing more than an elaborated version of the cube exercise in chapter 5.

Having initially worked out the three basic values of the source image, the student removed the friskets on the patterns of shadow on the main beams and the small shadows on the glazing bars and sprayed them with a dark tone (fig. 6.19). In some areas of the main shadow pattern, the darkness of this spray was subtly modulated to account for the occasional incidence of reflected light.

Then the two subtle shades of mid-gray were sprayed: first, the darker sections of the undersides of the beams and ring beams and the patterned shadow on the wall; second, the softer value on the undersides of all planes (fig. 6.20).

Finally, all the remaining underside planes on the beams and the shaded planes of the glazing bars were exposed and sprayed with a slightly lighter gray tone (fig. 6.21). However, as always when airbrushing darker shaded planes, these are sprayed not in a regular manner, but in subtly alternating pulses of light and dark to simulate the shimmer of reflected light along their length.

This illustration required just one frisket and, like all the illustrations previously discussed, the airbrush procedure was based upon a critical evaluation of the tonal structure of the selected image.

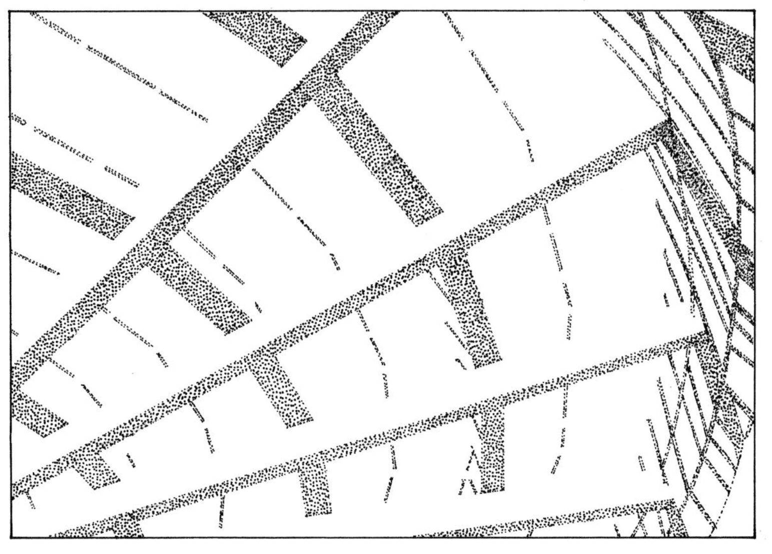

6.20 Atrium airbrushing sequence: Step 2

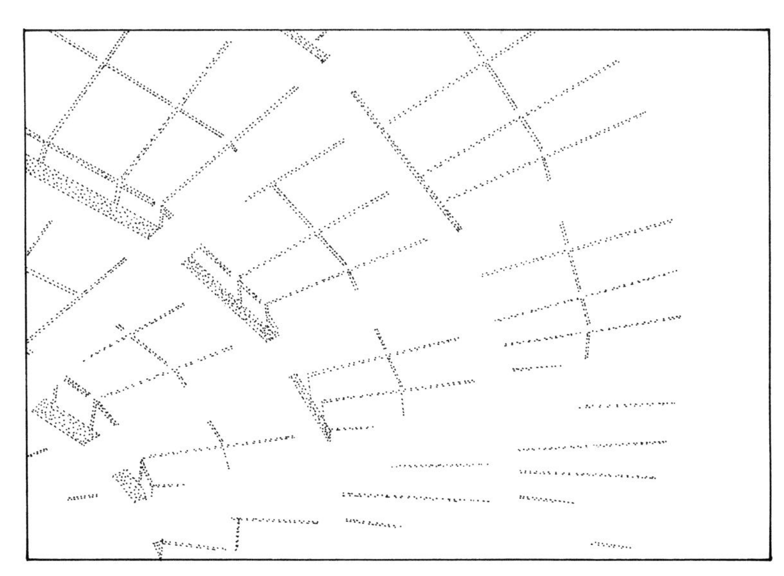

6.21 Atrium airbrushing sequence: Step 3

Exercise: Light Studies

Acrylic on illustration board,
8 x 8 in (20 x 20 cm)

This exercise (fig. 6.22) is based on the observation of the various patterns and qualities of value produced by light as it washes across architectural planes. Harnessing the airbrush medium to the way we perceive the pattern of light, the exercise also aims to sharpen your perception of the minutia of the visual experience.

Carefully select four details of different light effects in and on buildings. Focus exclusively on the quality of the light rather than on the architecture itself.

This page and next:
6.22 Four light studies

Outline the pattern of shade and shadow within an 8 x 8 in (20 x 20 cm) square on illustration board. Cover the image in frisket film, and trace-cut the pattern of lines. Then, with the airbrush loaded with lampblack, spray basic ascending dark-to-light values. (This project may require replacing some friskets or adding new ones.)

Doing an exercise like this will help you master the delicacy of spraytone value effects, an important airbrush skill. Concentrate on the subtle differentiation of values and on the interplay between hard-edged tones and diffuse patches of shade.

The examples shown are four student versions of this project.

6.23 Sundeck at Seaside, Florida

DEMONSTRATION:
Sundeck at Seaside, Florida

Watercolor on illustration board,
22 x 30 in (56 x 76 cm)

Two colors, lampblack and ultramarine, were used for this illustration (fig. 6.23). The spraying of the structural tracery of the sundeck used three values of black: a soft black, a midtone gray, and a light gray. The sundeck portion of the illustration was achieved with a single frisket. All color changes require an additional frisket; in this case, a second frisket was used to introduce the blue of the sky.

First, an outline drawing was carefully traced from the projected image of a 35 mm slide taken on a photo-assignment visit to Seaside, Florida, on the Gulf of Mexico. The whole surface was covered with a frisket.

The sundeck was then airbrushed in three ascending value stages, following the tonal steps established in the cube exercise in chapter 5 (that is, dark values airbrushed before midtones, and midtones before light values). All the dark shadows and shade on the sundeck and canopy, the line of shadow along the protruding lip of the deck, and the underside joints in its boarding were cut, exposed, and sprayed first. Then the dark gray underside planes were cut, exposed, and sprayed in a mid-gray. Finally, a light gray tone was sprayed on the shaded, vertical planes. This three-stage rendering process is best illustrated by the three values on the flags (fig. 6.24).

Then the frisket protecting the flagpole was removed and, to simulate its line of shade, a hairline pass of soft gray was sprayed. To keep the line straight, the student ran the airbrush nozzle along the tilted edge of a metal straightedge.

Leaving the paper border around the frisket in position, the student cleared the remaining bits of frisket in preparation for the final stage. A new sheet of frisket was then applied to the entire image and trace-cut so that only the sky (both around the outside of the deck and between the slats of wood) was exposed. An ultramarine blue fade was then applied to the sky using a buildup of horizontal passes fading downward from dark to light.

Once the second frisket was removed and the illustration revealed, the student used a technical pen to add the lines of the wire balustrading, bolts, and bracket securing the top of the flagpole to the gable.

Two points concerning this demonstration are worth noting. The first relates to the three-step tonal airbrushing of the sundeck. Within each value stage exists the possibility for introducing tonal variation. These variations can be detected in different regions of this illustration, such as the back of the armchair and the deck cornerpost. These minor shifts in values, as well as rendering reflected light in the shadows and shade, animate the values and bring life to the illustration.

Second, the student adjusted the composition immediately after the drawing stage. Once the outline of the drawing was traced from the slide projection, the student decided that a more balanced composition could be achieved if the lower section of the drawing was cropped.

6.24 Flags showing the three value steps

A common misconception about the airbrush is that it is a time-consuming medium. This is a myth. The illustrations in this chapter took between 30 and 60 minutes. The most time-consuming part of the process is finding the source image and planning the spraying sequence. But this stage becomes faster with experience. Even the painstaking practice of replacing friskets to protect previously sprayed areas can be kept to a minimum, allowing you to reduce both time and expense.

7 The Photocopy Frisket Technique

7.1 Gluing the photocopy to the frisket

A shortcut airbrush technique that is extremely popular with architecture students completely eliminates the drawing stage, allowing the illustrator to move directly to airbrushing. This shortcut relies on a photocopy of a photograph of a building or model as its starting point, and opens up a range of rendering possibilities.

First, select a source photograph that is fairly simple and free from heavily textured surfaces. Then make two photocopies of the image, resizing it if necessary. The first photocopy will act as a reference during the spraying phase, and the second as a surrogate drawing. Affix the second photocopy directly to the face of a sheet of frisket film using a heavy-duty aerosol spray adhesive, such as photo spray mount (fig. 7.1). Note that aerosol adhesive is a hazardous product and must always be used in a well-ventilated area or, whenever possible, outdoors. Then place the image face up on top of a sheet of illustration board (be sure to use a robust surface support, such as Crescent illustration board No. 110), and peel away the frisket sheet backing to laminate the image to the board (fig. 7.2).

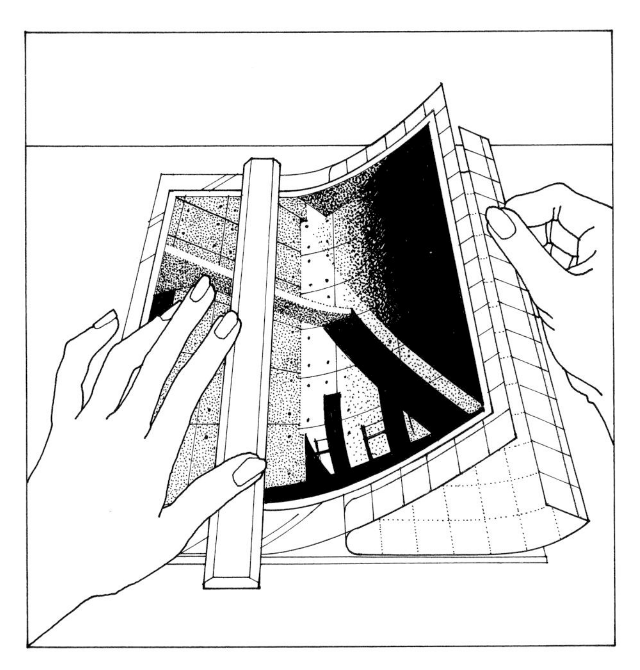

7.2 Laminating the photocopy frisket to the illustration board

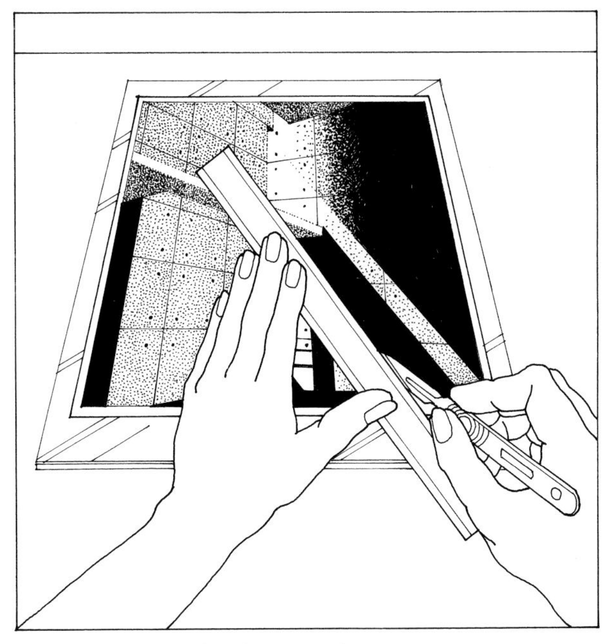

7.3 Trace-cutting the photocopy frisket

Use the spare photocopy to work out the spraying sequence. Record in pencil the numbered sequence of spraying steps and, working from dark to light, the parts of the image that correspond to the ascending value scale.

With the laminated frisket firmly attached to the illustration board, begin cutting the frisket. In order to allow for a continuous spraying operation, trace-cut the entire image in one operation (fig. 7.3).

7.4 Tadao Ando's Church of the Light, Ibaraki, Japan

Demonstration: Tadao Ando's Church of the Light, Ibaraki, Japan

Watercolor, graphite, and Prismacolor on illustration board, 7 x 16 in (18 x 41 cm)

The source photograph for this illustration (fig. 7.4) was selected because it showed both subtle modulation of

7.5 Church of the Light airbrush sequence: Step 1

7.6 Church of the Light airbrush sequence: Step 2

shade and a diagonal shaft of strong sunlight. The shadow pattern exhibited both soft and hard edges, providing a marvelous vehicle for the airbrush medium.

Working with a preplanned strategy of five value spraying steps, the airbrushing sequence began after the frisket was removed from the darkest regions of the image. The chairs were sprayed first, followed by the dark wall on the far left, the small shadows, and the main shadow on the back wall that quickly fades as it approaches the source of light (fig. 7.5).

The next value step was the group of dark grays: the floor, the underside of the beam, and the ceiling (fig. 7.6). A small supplementary frisket was added and cut to protect the sunlit portion of the (fade on the) back wall from both the ceiling and the edge of the left-hand wall. First, the triangular patch of ceiling was exposed and sprayed (fig. 7.7).

Then the supplementary frisket and the photocopy frisket on the left-hand wall were removed, and a slightly lighter gray was sprayed (fig. 7.8). This was followed by the lighter, vertical plane of the beam (fig. 7.9) and, finally, the soft-toned fade descending to the floor on the sunlit portion of the back wall (fig. 7.10).

To complete the illustration, the stu-

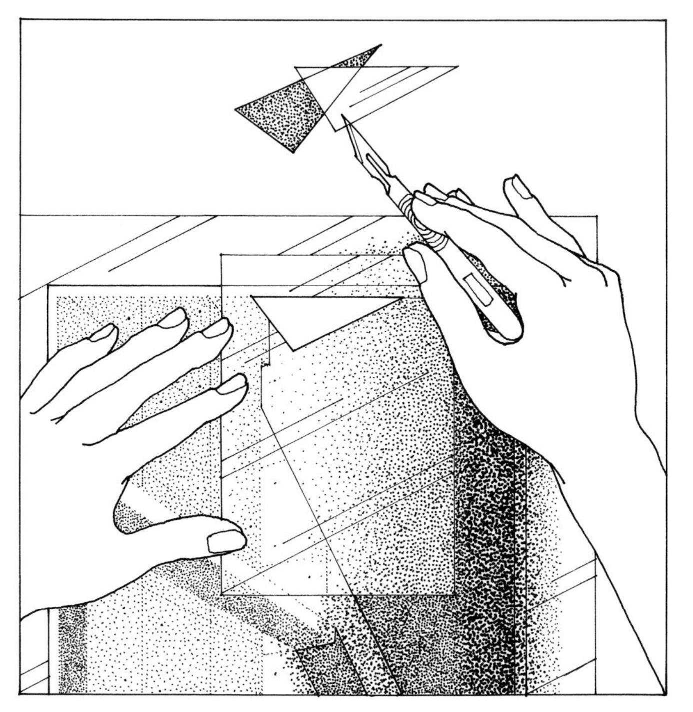

7.7 Protecting the fade

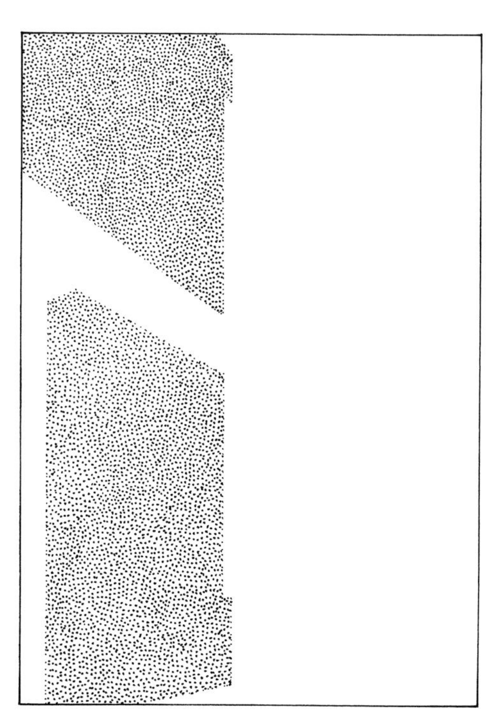

7.8 Church of the Light airbrush sequence: Step 3

7.9 Church of the Light airbrush sequence: Step 4

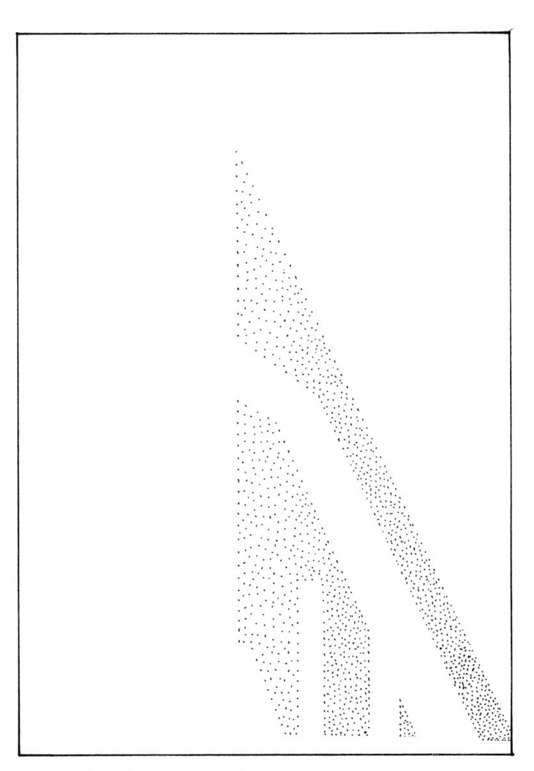

7.10 Church of the Light airbrush sequence: Step 5

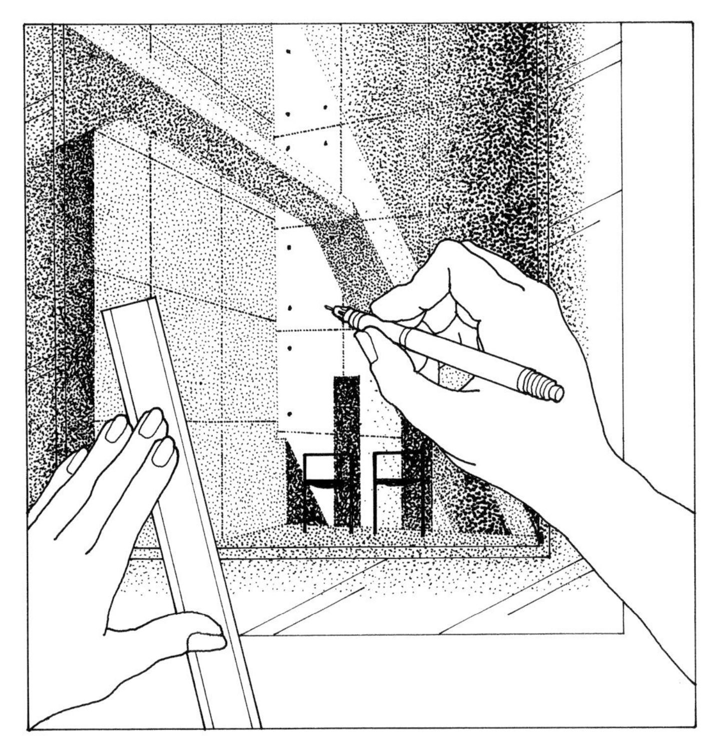
7.11 Adding detail in pencil

dent applied some detailed black and white pencilwork with the help of a straightedge to delineate the grid on the walls and the shadows of the studs (fig. 7.11).

Demonstration: Charles Gwathmey's Residence, Bridgehampton, New York

Watercolor, graphite, and Prismacolor on illustration board, 16 x 7 in (41 x 18 cm)

For this illustration (fig. 7.12), adjustments were made to the source image to improve the final composition. The student extended the width of the image to yield a more panoramic view of the landscape.

7.12 Charles Gwathmey's Residence, Bridgehampton, New York

After the photocopied image was spray mounted on the frisket film and laminated to the illustration board, all the dark openings and small areas of shadow were exposed and sprayed. The student then used a mixture of lamp-black and Payne's gray to spray the entire building façade. The foreground landscape elements were then unmasked and sprayed with a gradated spraytone of medium value with a darker emphasis at the outer reaches. Finally, the sky was exposed and built up to a dark spraytone that fades quickly as it descends to the skyline.

That such a dark backdrop spraytone could be incorporated on the now fully exposed illustration is explained by the fact that, after airbrushing was complete, the student subjected the dark value on the building façade to a controlled hatching with a white Prismacolor pencil. Applied both freehand and against a straightedge, this was introduced for three reasons: to simulate the effect of light catching the edges of the vertical timber cladding; to introduce highlights on the two upper curving portions of the façade; and, through lineweight, to emphasize the separation of value on the two main planes of the façade.

A freehand application of white Prismacolor and graphite adds the texture of grasses and the indication of mortar joints on the approach wall (fig. 7.13).

7.13 Adding detail in Prismacolor

The final illustration is part airbrush and part pencil drawing—the two techniques working in unison to create a very convincing rendition of this subtly textured and proportionally sensitive architecture.

7.14 Tadao Ando's Church on the Water, Hokkaido, Japan

7.15 Adding detail in ink

DEMONSTRATION:

Tadao Ando's Church on the Water, Hokkaido, Japan

Watercolor and ink on illustration board, 7 x 16 in (18 x 41 cm)

This illustration (fig. 7.14) also demonstrates how a combination of different mark-making techniques can be used to achieve delicate textures, patterns, or surface details that are far too intricate for the airbrush medium. To enhance the difference between the hard-edged architectural forms and the softness of the setting, reflections and ripples in the water were added in freehand penwork (fig. 7.15). The spare photocopy was used as a reference to elaborate in freehand the edges of the landscape and the silhouettes of the trees.

DEMONSTRATION:

Ricardo Legorreta's House, Sonoma County, California

Acrylic on illustration board,
11 x 11½ in (28 x 29 cm)

Two friskets were used for this illustration (fig. 7.16)—an initial photocopy frisket and a supplementary frisket to protect the airbrushed building from the transparent royal blue sprayed on the sky area. The student accidentally oversprayed the top portion of the sky, causing a dark, patchy hue. To rescue his illustration, the student used strips of 3-inch=wide (8 cm) Scotch tape to completely mask everything but the top sky area. With the illustration board tilted into a sink, this area was then gently washed out with water applied with a moist cloth. Once the value of the blue was softened, it was allowed to dry. Then the student sprayed it with a light spraytone of acrylic white until it matched the value of the lower, framed area of sky seen through the building.

Although successful in this case, this was a risky procedure: the student broke two basic rules. First, it is not recommended that areas of paint, especially on illustration board, be washed away on an illustration. Second, Scotch tape should never be applied to illustration board as it can pluck away its surface. Scotch tape does have a masking function, but only when using brush-applied washes on the more robust watercolor papers (see page 98).

7.16 Ricardo Legorreta's Sonoma County, California house

Knowing this, the student took the risk that those parts of the illustration it protected might later pull away. Fortunately, the illustration survived with little obvious damage. However, if the illustration had been airbrushed on softer hot-pressed illustration board, it would have been completely unrescuable.

7.17 Eaves and window

7.18 Eaves detail

Demonstration: **Eaves and Window**

Watercolor and Prismacolor on watercolor paper, 8 x 10 in (20 x 25 cm)

This delicate illustration (fig. 7.17) results from the simple process of cutting and exposing the image in the ascending sequence of dark to light values. The power of this image lies in its utter simplicity: the pattern of straight and curved shadows created by the corrugated roof, cladding, and venetian blinds. The subtlety of this image is exemplified by the attention to the soft range of grays. For instance, reflected light is indicated in the main shadow cast by the eave; two shades of gray were used to describe the shade and shadow of the cladding; white Prismacolor was used to delineate the horizontal divisions of the shaded portions of the venetian slats; and the undulations in the corrugated roof were represented in masterly fashion. The student achieved the soft, subdued quality of this illustration by using watercolor paper, which is more absorbent than the harder, smoother illustration board.

Demonstration: **Eaves Detail**

Watercolor on illustration board, 6 x 7 in (15 x 18 cm)

This small-scale roof detail is a little gem of an airbrush illustration (fig. 7.18). What is so unusual about this image is that the student neglected to fade and blend the halftone shades on the curved faces of the eave support brackets—an oversight that lent a starkness of value reminiscent of a faceted gemstone.

DEMONSTRATION: **Column of Light**

Watercolor on illustration board,
12 x 16 in (30 x 41 cm)

To create this illustration (fig. 7.19), the student airbrushed everything except the column, its capital, and the shutter in a dark-to-light sequence, beginning with the dark bands of shadow and the window apertures, and working through the four values to end with the soft gray tones on the mullions, window frame, and between the uppermost beams.

The student then removed all the residual photocopy frisket and, using the spare photocopy as a guide, penciled in the outlines of shadows on the column and capital, as well as those defining the planes of the shutter louvers.

The illustration was then completely recovered with a new sheet of frisket film and the column, the shutter, and the main shadows on the capital and column were trace-cut. These areas were then exposed and airbrushed. To simulate the column's light-catching curve, the shadows on the column were allowed to quickly fade at the edges. The two bands of molding below the capital at the head of the column were exposed next and given their respective soft spraytones. Finally, the column was fully exposed to receive two vertical bands of faint spraytone on each side.

The column then was reprotected with a supplementary frisket so that the shutter could be worked on. The diagonal shadow and the series of louver shadows were exposed and sprayed. Then the airbrush was cleaned and the color cup replenished with Winsor green. Using the same dark-to-light strategy, the student cut and sprayed the three values of green on the shutter.

7.19 Column of light

This illustration exploits the sharp quality of sunlight as it flickers across the fretwork of the timber façade. Its potency comes from a full exploitation of the figure-ground relationship and an interplay between equal amounts of positive and negative space.

Although the photocopy frisket technique greatly expedites the production of professional-looking illustrations, it is unwise to rely exclusively on its use. It is better used as an auxiliary tool, as the immediacy of the process diminishes the important act of drawing and the freedom to develop your own compositions.

8 Shedding Light on Orthographics

Light is central to our visual perception of architecture; light is the medium by which we see its form. Le Corbusier described architecture as "the magnificent play of masses brought together in light." Louis Kahn put it more poetically when he said: "All the material in nature, the mountains and the streams and the air, and we, are made of light which has been spent, and this crumpled mass called material casts a shadow, and the shadow belongs to light."

One of the main advantages of the airbrush is its ability to render the subtle behavior of light in all its forms. Light, shade, and shadows indicate depth, volume, surface quality, and inclination of plane. Therefore, the effects of light provide important visual information about both actual spaces and forms and pictorial illustrations of them.

Other cues indicating depth include overlap (when a portion of one object in the field of view partially hides another), relative size or convergence (when objects appear to decrease in size as their distance from the viewer increases), atmospheric haze or aerial perspective (when objects closer to the viewer appear clearer or sharper than those in the distance), and position in field (when objects higher in the field of view appear farther away than those in the lower portion of the field of view).

When we draw a perspective, we utilize many or all of these pictorial depth cues to create a convincing illusion of space. Orthographic drawings, however, are essentially flat and diagrammatic in nature, making it difficult for nonarchitects to visualize depth in the drawing. Still, orthographic drawings lie at the heart of architectural design and its communication. Consequently, some architects elaborate their drawings—especially those intended for public consumption—with value and color in order to increase their spatial readability and to clarify the relationship between interior and exterior space.

The two key depth cues available to

orthographic drawings are light (plus its shade and shadow) and atmospheric haze. The major contributor to the illusion of depth is, of course, light. To bring light into orthographic drawings you must airbrush all the values (shade and shadow) that result from its presence. In other words, to illustrate light you record its absence. Thus, a two-dimensional diagram can be transformed into the illusion of a three-dimensional space—one that can be inhabited visually. Shadows in plans should first be drawn in pencil to a length corresponding to the scaled height of the cutting plane. After the frisket is cut and removed to expose them, shadows are airbrushed to emphasize their extremities. As usual, establish the darkest portions first and use controlled passes to render the tones. This spatial illusion can be further emphasized by a subtle technique in which a narrow band of value is inserted along the shadow side of all the wall planes and, when possible, along the edges farthest from the light sources of forms within the plan. This tonal emphasis causes the white sectional cutting plane through the plan—and any objects that it may contain—to appear to pop out, creating the illusion that it occupies a space forward of the picture plane.

Atmospheric haze can be achieved through hierarchy of line weight. Sections can also be enhanced spatially by incorporating perspective views of the interior and exterior setting, causing a hybrid drawing known as a "section-perspective." Elevations can be enhanced by placing objects in front of and behind its plane. This creates a "pseudoperspective"—a composite elevation drawing that incorporates the powerful overlap depth cue.

Like all illustrations, orthographic drawings can, of course, only be airbrushed on a sufficiently durable surface. Mylar provides an excellent, robust airbrush surface, and its transparency allows for spraying on both the front and back of the sheet to create a layered value effect. As watercolor tends to be unstable on plastic surfaces, we recommended that acrylic paint be used.

The following illustrations show how the airbrush can be used to throw shadows on orthographic drawings (particularly the plan) and add other details that enhance the illusion of pictorial space, thereby making the drawings more spatially meaningful and accessible to a client's eye.

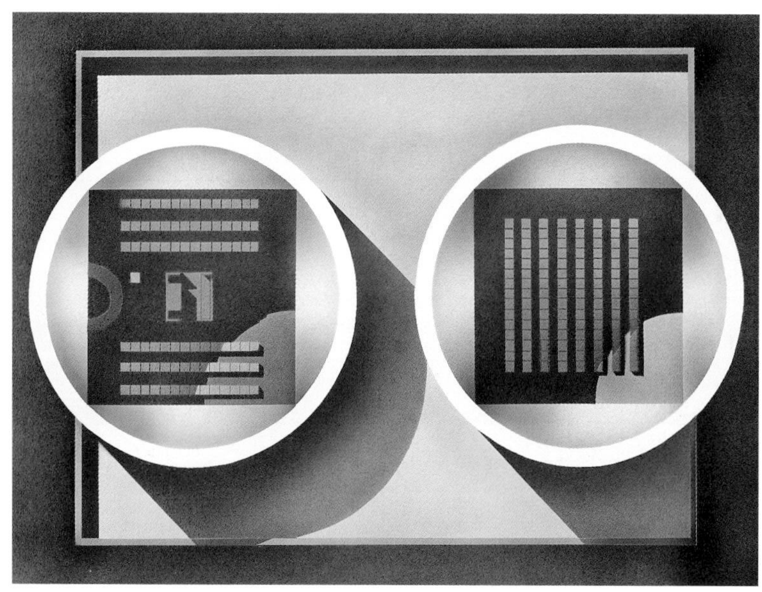

8.1 Ground floor and roof level plans for Mario Botta's Cymbalista Synagogue, Tel Aviv

DEMONSTRATION:

Ground Floor and Roof Level Plans for Mario Botta's Cymbalista Synagogue, Tel Aviv

Acrylic on illustration board,
11 x 14 in (28 x 36 cm)

These two plans (fig. 8.1) show how airbrushed shade and shadows can be used to enhance the visual impact of orthographic drawings. In each case the preliminary outline drawing was covered completely with frisket film and then trace-cut in one operation. The spraying sequence started with the exposure of all the areas of black, followed by the fade (more apparent on the roof plan) on the cast shadows. Then the two next-lightest grays were sprayed in turn. Theoretically both plans could have been airbrushed using one frisket, but the student decided to use a supplementary frisket after the main body of the drawing was airbrushed. It was applied to the lower section of the roof plan in order to add two bands of shadow on the parapet, and, where necessary, to make tonal adjustments. Finally, various lines describing the modules of seats, steps, etc., were added with a pencil against a straightedge.

The horizontal sectional slice in both illustrations was left unsprayed to intensify the impression of three-dimensionality through high contrast. While conforming to the conventions of the plan, the result is a powerful, dramatic optical illusion that communicates three-dimensional space. Moreover, these illustrations encourage the viewer to peer into the depicted space rather than simply look at them.

Demonstration:

Section of Mario Botta's Cymbalista Synagogue, Tel Aviv

Acrylic on illustration board,
20 x 23½ in (51 x 60 cm)

This illustration (fig. 8.2) is taken from the physical model for a Mario Botta design. Again, the aim was to maximize the illusion of depth using the shades and, especially, fades of shadows from the rooflights against the inverted cones of the two chambers.

Two basic friskets were used for this sectional view. The first allowed airbrushing of the interiors of the two chambers. After the first frisket was removed, a second was applied and the background area cut and exposed to allow for the application of the fade.

With the second frisket still in place, selected areas of foreground detail—especially around the skylights and the furniture along the groundline—were exposed to receive some detail work. This necessitated the introduction of supplementary friskets.

The range of values in the composition of the spraytones is key to the powerful sense of implied depth in this illustration. This tonal structure exploits both high and low contrast that responds to the three zones of foreground, middle ground, and background. For example, the high contrast between the white cutting plane and the dark adjacent spraytones emphasizes the nearness of the sectional slice as it appears

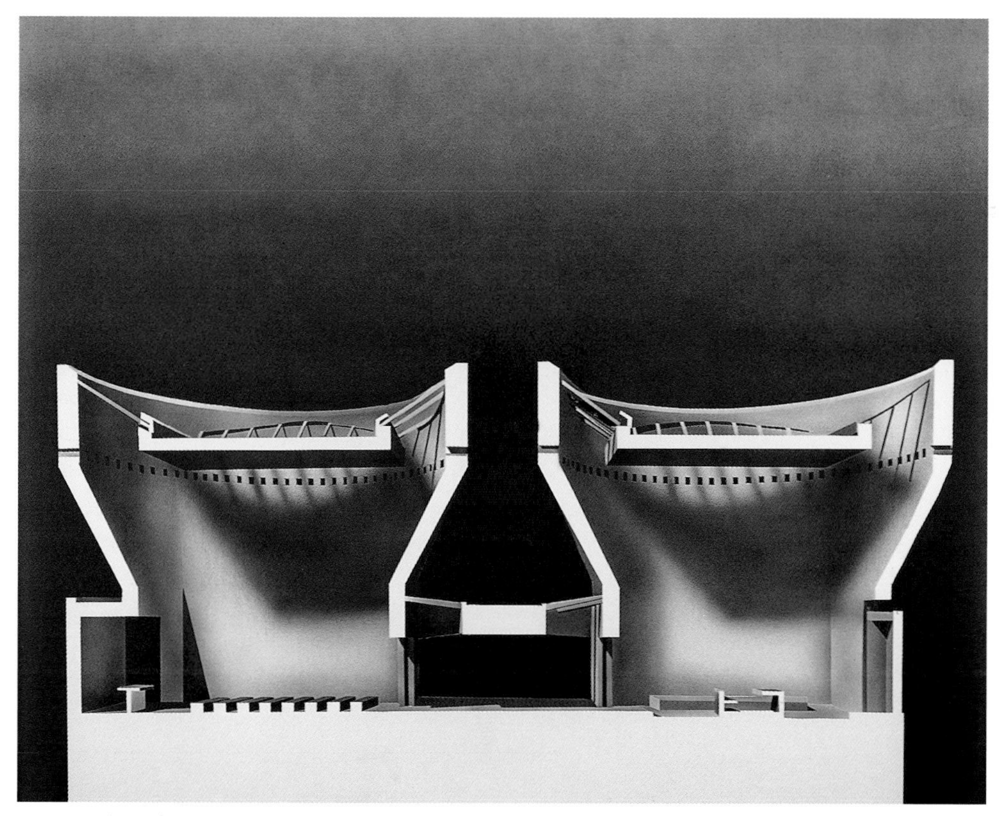

8.2 Section of Mario Botta's Cymbalista Synagogue, Tel Aviv

on the picture plane (foreground). The modulated values inside the two chambers represent interior space as occurring behind the cutting plane (middle ground). Finally, the dark backdrop fade simulates atmospheric space behind the building (background), effectively pushing forward the architectural mass.

DEMONSTRATION: **Patkau Architects' Barnes House, Namaino, British Columbia**

Acrylic on illustration board,
11 x 14 in (28 x 36 cm)

Conventionally, shadows in plans are projected at 45 degrees from a single light source (see fig. 8.1). But an interesting, radical departure is to show sunlight flooding into a plan from all sides —a condition that, possibly, is closer to actual experience. This illustration (fig. 8.3) demonstrates the effectiveness of this strategy.

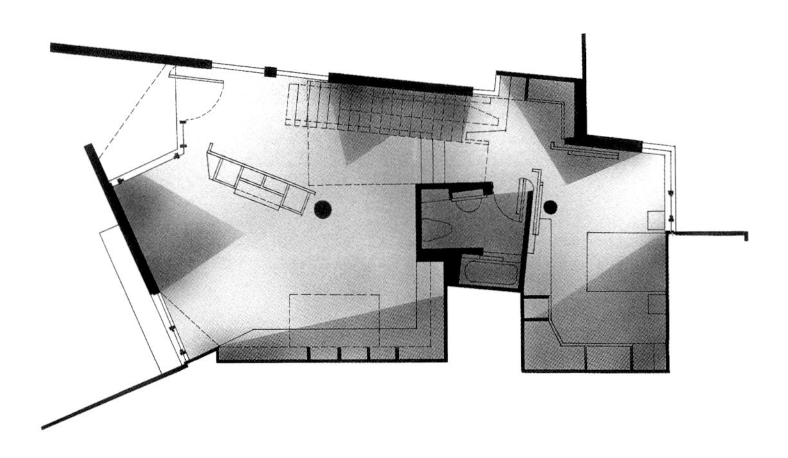

8.3 Patkau Architects' Barnes House, Namaino, British Columbia

DEMONSTRATION: **Elevation of Richard Meier's Royal Dutch Paper Mills Headquarters, Hilversum, Netherlands**

Acrylic on illustration board,
15 x 18 in (38 x 46 cm)

Like plans and sections, elevations conventionally exist as flat diagrams on the picture plane. However, they can be transformed dramatically by the introduction of space, becoming what is known as pseudoperspectives. This is done by assuming a background zone behind the elevation and a foreground zone between the plane of the elevation and the viewer.

This illustration (fig. 8.4) is an example of an elevation converted into a pseudoperspective. It exploits the effect of shadows cast at 45 degrees from an upper-left-hand light source. A walkway in the foreground gives a strong illusion of space in front of the elevation. In fact, the architectural form appears to be a building occupying a spatial setting, the illusion being intensified by the backdrop sky and a simulation of a distant landscape.

Created using the techniques already demonstrated, this illustration was completed with the addition of some light pencil delineation on the façade. The foreground, sky, and background were airbrushed last. The distant landscape effect was achieved with a simple hand-held mask—a torn strip of bond paper. With the building and border protected, a portion of the tear was held slightly above the surface of the artwork (to create a soft edge) and a light spraytone airbrushed from the torn edge down to the lower border. Then a different portion of the mask was held just above the first position and a second layer of spraytone was applied. The overlapping sequence of spraytones continued upward two more times. This simple masking creates a layered diffusion along the skyline—the progressively darker values of nearer layers of landscape simulating the atmospheric haze illusion we associate with distance.

The torn-paper technique can also be used to simulate foliage—the paper being torn to create a more meandering edge (fig. 8.5). This technique was used in the illustration on page 92.

Liquid frisket can also be used to simulate foliage before a sky spraytone is airbrushed. This effect is also easy to create. Gently apply small dabs of masking fluid to the region of the treeline using a small piece of natural sponge. After the fluid is dry, and the skyline protected, the foliage can be sprayed. Rubbing away the liquid frisket will reveal a light filigree foliage (see illustrations on page 18).

8.4 Elevation of Richard Meier's Royal Dutch Paper Mills Headquarters, Hilversum, Netherlands

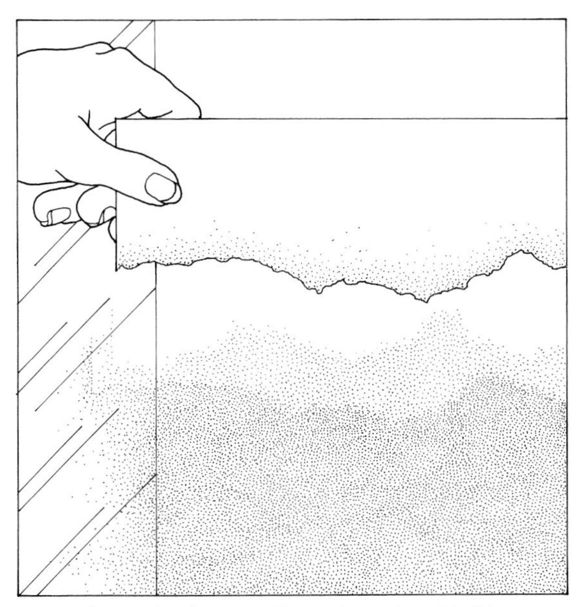

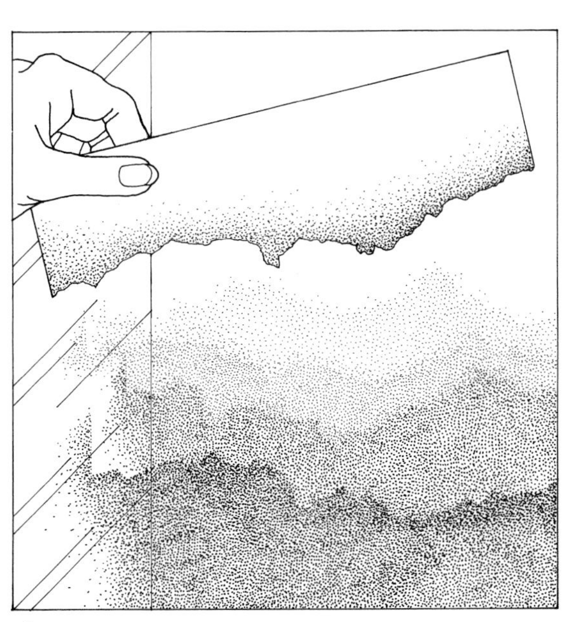

8.5 A distant landscape effect using a hand-held torn-paper mask

8.6 Sectional perspective for residential interior, Goshen, Arkansas

DEMONSTRATION:

Sectional Perspective for Residential Interior, Goshen, Arkansas

Acrylic on illustration board,
30 x 40 in (76 x 102 cm)

An even stronger illusion of depth can be achieved when the coordinates of one-point perspective are projected to a vanishing point located inside the cutting plane of the section. Target the vanishing point to provide the optimum viewing angle, and make sure the projected lines of convergence intersect the inside corners of the cutting plane. This will produce a hybrid drawing with the full gamut of depth cues.

Initially drawn in pencil on a 24 x 30 in (61 x 76 cm) sheet of vellum, the perspective drawing for this illustration (fig. 8.6) was enlarged and photocopied on bond paper. The photocopy was then mounted onto frisket film using photo spray adhesive, applied to the surface of illustration board, and trace-cut.

The building interior was airbrushed first, the initial spraying sequences establishing the shifting values of shade on the walls, ceiling, and floor. The more intricate features in the interior, such as the chairs and the spiral staircase, required supplementary friskets.

To allow for general, corrective adjustments to the interior, the board was cleared of all residual pieces of mask and a new full frisket applied. Additional airbrushing darkened the tone on the ceiling, softened the edges of some shadows and intensified and sharpened others, and generally emphasized the overall contrast between the interior and the white cutting plane.

A second full frisket was then applied to protect the building while the background was airbrushed in Payne's gray. After the sky spraytone fade was built up (darker at the top to emphasize the white of the sectional slice), the layered landscape was sprayed using the hand-held torn-paper masking technique. To complete the illustration, pencil linework was used to indicate the pattern of floorboards and overhead lighting cables.

The illustrations in this chapter are examples of student experimentation with the airbrush on a basic array of architectural presentation drawings. There are, of course, many other applications, such as the introduction of selective areas of value or color to existing line drawings. For example, skies can be dropped behind sections and elevations, floor plans and site plans can be color-coded or spatially embellished using color and shadow projection, and the surfaces of models can be airbrushed with detail.

Yet another application is the airbrushing of photographs of architectural models taken at eye level. This technique minimizes the "toytown" appearance of model photographs, communicating a strong sense of reality at human scale. The illustration in figure 8.7, based on a photograph of a model for an extension for a school building, is an excellent example of this. Rendered in acrylic on illustration board (15 x 24 in [38 x 61 cm]), it gives the impression not of a scale model but rather of an existing building.

The real potential of the airbrush in orthographic drawing and architectural presentation is to provide greater spatial resolution to conventional line drawings. While line allows us to perceive edge and contour, value (light, shade, and shadow) directly communicates mass, negative space, and quality of surface. The addition of this information to traditional orthographic drawings not only makes them more visually appealing, but also gives viewers (especially clients) a better understanding of the architecture they represent.

8.7 Illustration based on a photograph of Terence O'Rourke's model for an extension of a school building, London

9 Advanced Image-Building: Multiple Friskets

After mastering the basic exercises and achieving confidence comes the advanced stage in airbrushing, when we encourage you to find your own subject matter, freely experiment with the medium, and develop a personal means of achieving sprayed images using multiple masks.

Of course, captivating illustrations cannot be achieved through masterly airbrush technique alone—they rely on formally solid, compositionally interesting initial drawings. This requires careful consideration, selection, and manipulation of the source image. The illustrations in this chapter (with the exception of the first two) were created as part of a mini-workshop that rigorously discussed the viability of images in terms of visual engagement. The workshop followed a photo assignment in which students took photographs of visually interesting architectural events. Their slides were projected and critiqued by the group, each image being thoroughly analyzed in terms of content, degree of visual interest (its power to capture and retain the attention of the eye), compositional balance, and possible improvement through modification or cropping.

Symmetrical compositions—central vanishing points in perspective views or an equal balance of forms—were avoided, as they tend to be dull and predictable. Instead, off-center arrangements that counterbalanced graphic elements of unequal weight and dissimilar size were favored.

The group also discussed the images' message areas and visual contrast. "Message area" refers to the part of the illustration in which the meaning of the image is conveyed. This zone is also referred to as the "center of interest" or the "focal point." As the main function of the human eye is to detect movement and change in the field of view, the eye is immediately drawn to regions of greater contrast. Thus, visual interest in an illustration is created through a controlled use of contrast: contrasting levels of information and detail, and contrast in size, value, scale, etc., of graphic components. Therefore, message areas usually coincide with and are signaled by the area of greatest contrast.

Graphic contrast is signaled by the value patterns—i.e., the pattern of light and dark described in chapter 6 and discussed further in chapter 8. A good way of assessing the abstract potential of an illustration is to project the slide upside down. This allows the viewer to disengage from the image's content and concentrate solely on the essential structure of the composition.

9.1 Tectonic kit of parts

EXERCISE:
Tectonic Kit of Parts

Watercolor on illustration board,
22 x 30 in (56 x 76 cm)

To consolidate many of the spraying effects previously covered, we start with an exercise that involves airbrushing directly from a white wooden model. This subject matter provides a sophisticated version of the earlier cube, cylinder, and sphere exercises.

The preparatory drawing for this illustration (fig. 9.1) was made directly from the model, which was placed in strong sunlight against a white foamcore base and backdrop. Once the pencil-drawing, frisket-covering, and frisket-cutting stages were complete, the sequence of airbrushing the tonal steps began. First, the deepest shadows were sprayed (fig. 9.2). Then the shaded areas, beginning with the dark recesses, the shaded columns seen through the apertures (fig. 9.3), and finally the slightly lighter, modulated shades on the side planes were established (fig. 9.4).

9.2 Tectonic kit of parts airbrushing sequence: Step 1

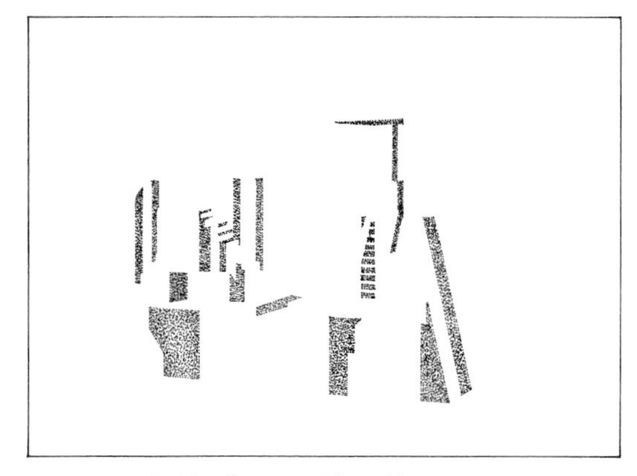

9.3 Tectonic kit of parts airbrushing sequence: Step 2

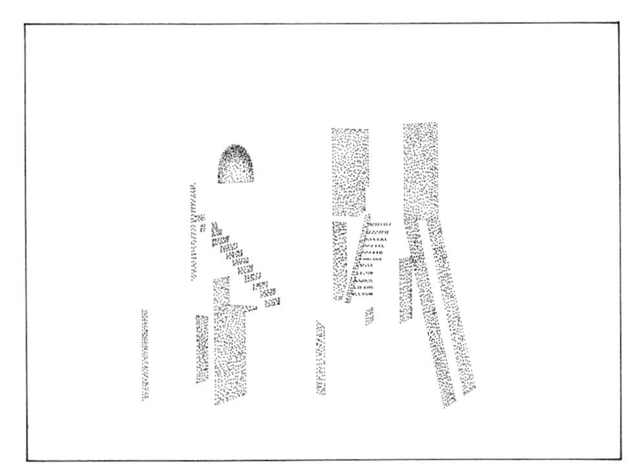

9.4 Tectonic kit of parts airbrushing sequence: Step 3

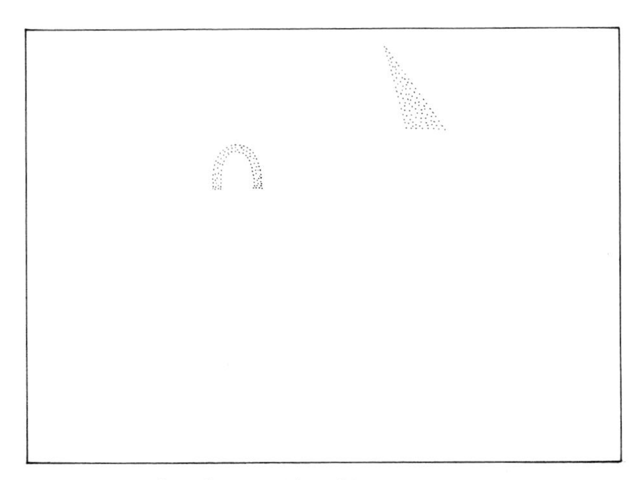

9.5 Tectonic kit of parts airbrushing sequence: Step 4

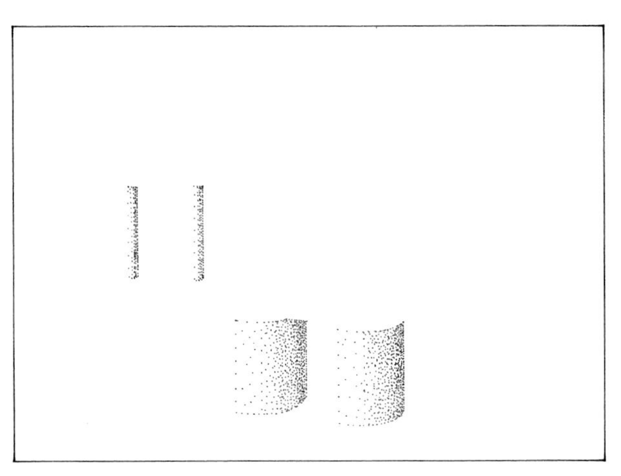

9.6 Tectonic kit of parts airbrushing sequence: Step 5

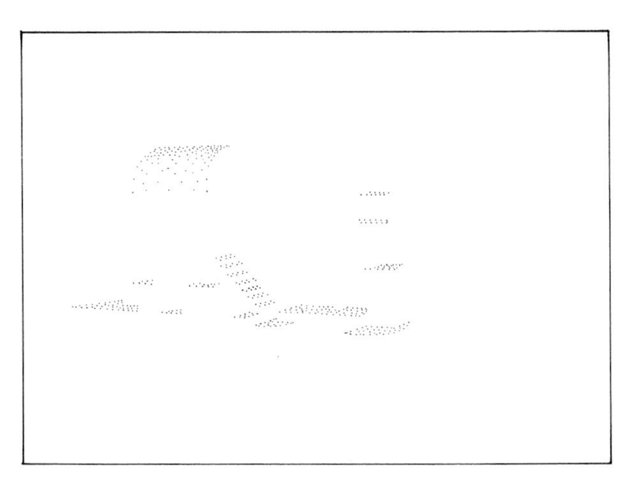

9.7 Tectonic kit of parts airbrushing sequence: Step 6

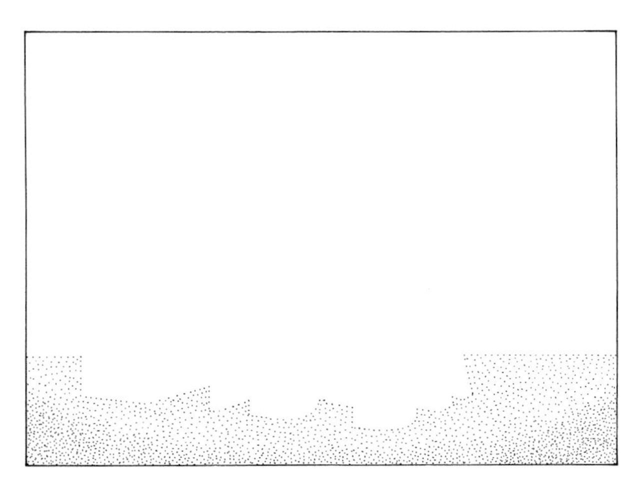

9.8 Tectonic kit of parts airbrushing sequence: Step 7

9.9 Tectonic kit of parts airbrushing sequence: Step 8

9.10 Tectonic kit of parts (color version)

The shaded side of the pyramid and the arched eave of the barrel roof were sprayed last (fig. 9.5).

The two cylinders and the two columns were sprayed early in this phase—their vertical faces exposed and, to emphasize their roundness, their drums carefully modeled in a buildup of vertical passes (fig. 9.6). Then both cylinders were refrisketed in order to protect their highlights from subsequent overspray and, especially, from the spraytone which would later be applied to their upper edge. Finally, all the lighter values (occurring mainly on the horizontal planes of the volumes and on the barrel roof) received their delicate tones (fig. 9.7).

Next, all the remaining frisket was removed and replaced with a fresh sheet. The foreground plane was trace-cut and exposed to receive first a pale spraytone and then a spatter effect (fig. 9.8). Once dry, the foreground area was remasked before the frisket on the background was cut and removed. After a color change to cobalt blue, this was subjected to a bluish fade (fig. 9.9).

The student who executed this illustration also made a four-frisket color version of the same illustration using cadmium red, permanent sap green, Winsor blue, and lampblack (fig. 9.10).

9.11 Petroleum tanks, St. Mark's, Florida

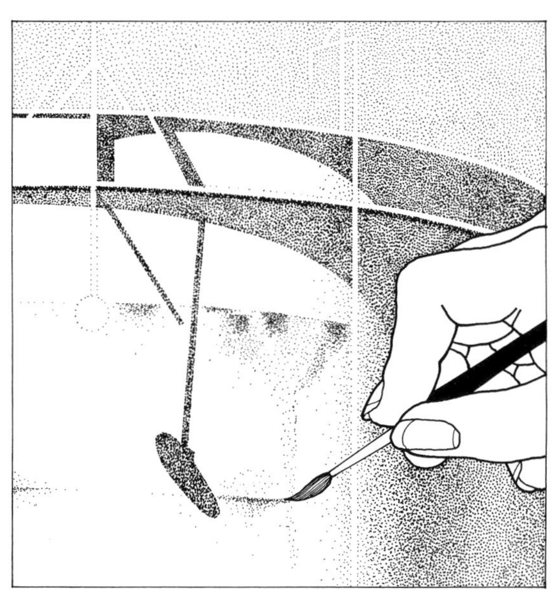

9.12 The brush-applied wet-on-wet technique

DEMONSTRATION:

Petroleum Tanks, St. Mark's, Florida

Watercolor on watercolor paper,
22 x 30 in (56 x 76 cm)

The preliminary pencil outline drawing for this illustration (fig. 9.11) was made on the textured surface of 140 lb rough watercolor paper. Watercolor paper was selected for this project because a major portion of the image required a paintbrush-applied watercolor treatment. Frisket film was not used because it would have allowed the liquid paint to creep under its edges. Instead, a 3 in (8 cm) wide strip of Scotch tape, a more resilient and waterproof mask, was employed. As watercolor paper has a robust surface, it is able to receive an extremely high-tack mask without damage to its surface.

The initial step involved the introduction of the texture of rust on the upper sunlit part of the main petroleum tank—a texture requiring a technique called "wet-on-wet," in which paint is applied to a previously moistened surface (fig. 9.12). (The wet-on-wet technique involves a degree of chance, as the behavior of the paint cannot be strictly controlled. Therefore, before working directly on the artwork, try some trial runs to achieve this effect.) First, the entire image was protected with overlapping bands of Scotch tape, the overlapping creating a waterproof seal. Then all of the petroleum tank, except for the oilcan in the right foreground and the two thin bands at the top of the cylinder, were exposed. The tank was then subjected to an even wash of clean water applied with a paintbrush. With the wash still moist, flecks of burnt umber were dabbed on with a brush—the near-vertical position of the easel causing the paint to bleed and trickle down the still-wet surface.

With the wash dry and the central tank still exposed, the airbrush was used to spray the shaded fade on the right of the cylinder. With the surrounding Scotch tape still in place, the tank was then reprotected, this time with frisket film. (Frisket film is used because Scotch tape, if applied to previously airbrushed surfaces, will ruin the artwork. Therefore, use Scotch tape only on unsprayed watercolor paper and never over previously airbrushed parts of the artwork. Unlike frisket film, Scotch tape is unforgiving on sprayed artwork and, when removed, will not only pluck away the paint but also damage the paper surface.) This allowed the shadows cast from the pipework and the two bands at the top of the tank, as well as the main shadow from the neighboring tank, to be cut, exposed, and airbrushed to simulate the gradated effect of reflected light.

Next, the illustration was cleared of all Scotch tape and frisket film, and a new frisket film was applied over the entire surface. From this the three areas of deep shade and shadow on the left and right of the tanks and on the foreground plane were cut, removed, and airbrushed.

With the tank and the background still protected, the frisket on the foreground plane was removed. The completion of the foreground required two steps: first, an airbrushed spraytone to establish its pale base value, and second, the application of a variegated stipple created by dragging a knife across the paint-loaded bristles of an old toothbrush (fig. 9.13).

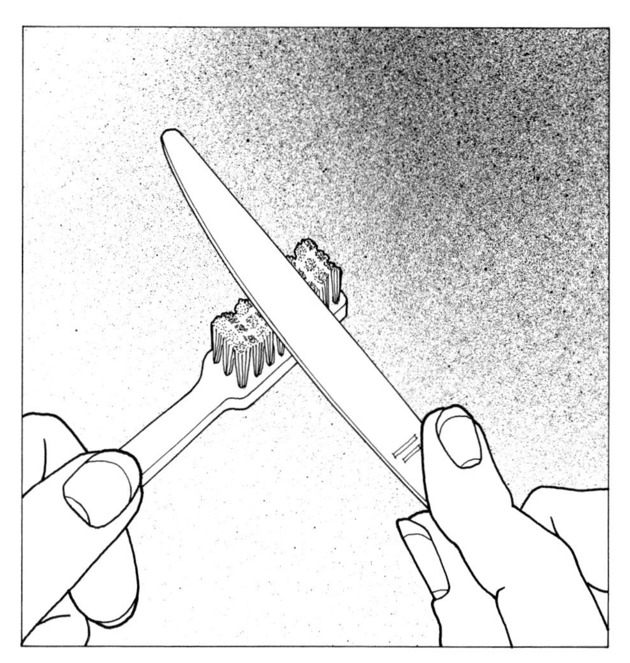

9.13 Spatter technique using a toothbrush

After the foreground was dry, all the remnants of frisket were removed and the entire image recovered. Then the oil-can was cut and sprayed in two stages in order to model its form. The skyline was trace-cut next, including the pipework that appears on its silhouette, and around the small area of foliage glimpsed between the two tanks. The foliage was exposed and then airbrushed using the hand-held mask technique described on pages 90–91, its darker value being blended into the lower area of the shadow. Finally, following a color change, the sky was exposed and its gradation airbrushed, its lower fade being allowed to overspray the treeline.

As noted earlier, this illustration would not have been possible if regular frisket film had been employed exclusively. Use Scotch tape on watercolor paper whenever you need to achieve

9.14 Petroleum tanks (second version)

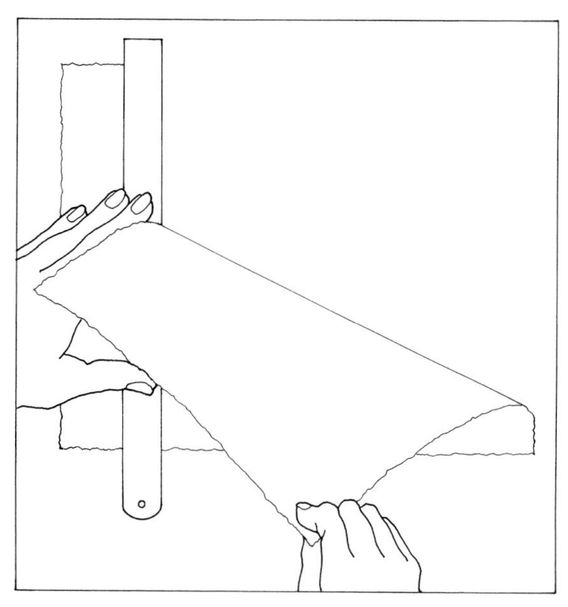

9.15 Tearing watercolor paper

highly textured effects, such as those found on weathered surfaces, and when you use a paintbrush to achieve this effect.

Note also that figure 9.11 comprises no more than four colors. When working with color it is important to understand the benefits of using a limited palette. Illustrations made with few colors tend to embody a self-imposed discipline—that is, a built-in harmonic that provides visual cohesion and has more impact on the eye. Rather than introducing new colors into the palette, try mixing the desired color from two or three already on hand. Many of the illustrations featured in this book derive from extremely economical color palettes.

Another illustration of the same subject matter is shown in figure 9.14. Although it appears more complicated, this image was created by the same airbrushing procedure used in the previous version. The main difference between the two was the intricate cutting of the initial Scotch tape mask to preserve the white pattern of the ladder.

Prior to the airbrushing stage, the watercolor paper of both illustrations was torn to the size of the intended artwork. The torn edge of this support is traditional in watercolor painting. It is achieved by tearing the paper against a straightedge held down firmly along the line of the tear (fig. 9.15).

DEMONSTRATION:
Santoríni

Watercolor on illustration board,
22 x 30 in (56 x 76 cm)

This illustration (fig. 9.16) combines two contrasting compositional elements: a sharply defined, sunlit foreground architecture, and a background of water and atmospheric diffusion. Each component demanded a subtly different airbrush approach.

After the image was totally masked in frisket film and trace-cut, airbrushing began in the lower region of the image, with all the darkest architectural shapes (the apertures of the windows and the small triangular-shaded planes of the walls) sprayed in black. Then, working from dark to light, the flat, domed, and curving planes were progressively exposed and subjected to either an even or gradated spraytone, exploiting any incidence of reflected light.

With the foreground value structure established, supplementary friskets were selectively used to spray the ochre door and the hint of soft color on various rooftops.

Once the foreground was finished, the architectural portion of the illustration was reprotected with frisket film and attention turned to the background ocean and sky. The two islands were cut from the original frisket and the one on the left exposed. This was airbrushed in two colors: ultramarine (green shade) and cerulean blue. These were sprayed to emphasize the darker coastline contour against the softer tone of the skyline. The right-hand island was exposed next and, using the same two blues, lightly airbrushed to achieve a softer, more distant-looking spraytone.

9.16 Santoríni

Then, after cutting around the silhouette of the buildings and along the visible portion of the horizonline, the ocean was exposed. To create a visual antidote to the hard-edged geometry of the architecture, the ocean was airbrushed first in a light spraytone of cerulean blue followed by ultramarine. These colors were freely applied using diagonal sweeps of the arm across the image. Closer attention was given to the lower right-hand corner to simulate the soft pattern of waves. This technique, in which colors are applied in the tradition of watercolor painting (that is, pockets of one transparent hue are superimposed and blended with previously applied areas of another hue), achieved the illusion of atmospheric haze.

The sky area was then exposed and airbrushed in a pale spraytone of cerulean blue with hints of ultramarine. During this final application, overspray was allowed to soften both the horizon line and the silhouettes of the two islands.

9.17 Gingerbread house, Quincy, Florida

DEMONSTRATION:
Gingerbread House, Quincy, Florida

Watercolor on illustration board,
22 x 30 in (56 x 76 cm)

Although seemingly intricate in detail, this illustration (fig. 9.17) results from a strategy involving four basic airbrushing zones: the shingle roof, the sky, the recessed portion of the façade, and the decorated gable. To economize on frisket film, the film was applied only to the areas being sprayed and the rest of the illustration was protected with sheets of bond paper held in place with drafting tape. Also, to avoid frisket flutter or prevent small pieces of film from becoming dislodged during airbrushing, the more intricate mask cutting was conducted in stages—that is, immediately before exposure and spraying.

Surrounded by its bond-paper mask, the roof plane was airbrushed first. The ridge tiles were cut, exposed, and modeled with the airbrush to achieve the illusion of roundness. The ridge was then reprotected before the horizontal shadow lines on the shingles were cut, exposed, and sprayed. These lines remained open while the vertical shadow lines—including those along the ridge tiles—were cut and revealed (fig. 9.18). This two-stage spraying sequence brought a greater depth of value to the horizontal shadow lines, corresponding to their darker value resulting from their more direct relationship to the angle of sunlight (fig. 9.19).

The shingle roof was finished after two more operations: a fine-grain, ran-

9.18 With the previously sprayed horizontal shadow lines left open, the vertical shingle shadow lines are cut and exposed.

9.19 The darkness of the horizontal shadow lines on the shingles appears to respond in value to the direction of sunlight.

9.20 The roof is completed with a toothbrush-applied stipple effect and a light, randomly airbrushed spraytone.

9.21 The recessed façade is completed in a two-stage operation that airbrushes the lines first and the main shadow second.

dom application of stipple created by flicking paint from a toothbrush, and a light, random spraytone airbrushed to create a variegated value effect (fig. 9.20).

The next step began after the initial mask was cleared away. The house was completely reprotected with bond paper and strips of frisket were placed around the area of the sky and cut to expose the sky. This was sprayed in an even, gentle tone of Winsor blue, which, to create an aura of light, quickly fades before it meets the edge of the roofline.

Then that mask was removed and a fresh frisket film was applied to the recessed part of the façade. Again, all remaining areas of the artwork were protected with a bond-paper mask. This region of the façade was airbrushed following two cutting sessions: the first to reveal and spray the dark pattern of lines and castellations on the cladding, the second to reveal and spray the more

9.22 The gable is completed first with shadow lines and then the soft spraytones on its decoration.

transparent body of shadow cast from the gable (fig. 9.21). All the remaining pieces of frisket were then removed.

With the surrounding artwork masked in paper, the decorated gable was protected with its own frisket film. Again, this was cut and airbrushed in two stages, the dark lines and crescents of shadows being exposed and sprayed before the softer spraytones (fig. 9.22).

Finally, to complete the illustration, an air eraser was used to create highlights on the tiny spheres and spindles on the gable. Loaded with cornstarch, the air eraser was aimed close to the artwork surface and the single-action trigger was depressed to release a short pulse of compound that etched the highlights.

Demonstration:
Peter Eisenman's Wexner Center, Columbus, Ohio

Watercolor on illustration board,
22 x 30 in (56 x 76 cm)

Composed almost entirely of flat surfaces and boxlike forms, this illustration (fig. 9.23) involved a straightforward airbrushing process. Its ease of achievement relied upon an analytical breakdown of the source photograph into its three main elements: freestanding gridwork, sky, and façades.

The potentially stark appearance of this image was softened somewhat both by the subtle mixing of lampblack, Payne's gray, cerulean blue, and Winsor blue in the color cup and by a "happy accident" when the overspray encroached on the more reflective surfaces in the composition.

With the first frisket protecting the entire outline drawing, airbrushing followed a cycle of cutting and exposure that first revealed the shaded underside planes of the freestanding gridwork and then the light-receiving planes (fig. 9.24). The latter were sprayed in a very soft tone of lampblack mixed with a tinge of Winsor blue to achieve a color that reflects the hue of the sky (fig. 9.25).

Then the image was cleared of the initial mask and refrisketed completely, and the negative space of the sky was cut and sprayed. This was airbrushed in two blues—a descending fade of cerulean blue that covered the entire sky, and an oversprayed fade of Winsor blue that covered the top portion of sky (fig. 9.26).

9.23 Peter Eisenman's Wexner Center, Columbus, Ohio

9.24 The shaded undersides of planes are airbrushed first.

9.25 With the shaded planes left open, the softer values of vertical planes are added.

9.26 Using a second frisket, the sky fade is achieved with two blues.

9.27 A third frisket protects the artwork while the glass and mullions are airbrushed in stages, allowing overspray on the panes of glass.

Next, a third replacement frisket was used and attention turned to the building façade in the left middle ground. A three-step cutting and spraying sequence first airbrushed the darker areas and shadows, and then exposed the fenestration glass and applied a spraytone mix of Payne's gray and lampblack. The third spraytone airbrushed the mullions in a lighter value of the same color mix; overspray was allowed to drift onto the still-exposed units of glass to encourage the effect of reflected and scattered light (fig. 9.27). However, the lines of shade on the mullions in this more detailed area of the illustration required a supplementary frisket. This was locally applied while the remaining parts of the image were protected with a bond-paper mask.

With much of the image still covered in frisket, the spraywork on the left-hand building façade was next protected with a bond-paper mask while attention turned to the façades of the lower-middle building. Fenestration glass was first exposed and sprayed using a dark mix of lampblack and Payne's gray. Finally, the grid of mullions was revealed to receive a slightly lighter-toned value of the same color mix (fig. 9.28).

The artwork was again stripped of all masks and protected with a fourth full-frisket film. All the outstanding darker areas cast onto the façade and the gridwork were airbrushed in lampblack (fig. 9.29). To provide a sense of depth, shadows were airbrushed in a subtle scale of value—darker in the foreground, lighter as they receded. Shadows were also variegated to simulate the quality of reflected light. Also, this fourth frisket provided an opportunity to adjust the previously airbrushed shadows on the building façade.

In this illustration, the basic function of the airbrush—that is, to deliver a controlled and atomized mist of paint to the surface—is exploited fully. A subtle mixing of color and a controlled overspray were used to simulate the refraction of tiny particles of light as they scatter across the surfaces of smooth, reflective architectural planes. It is this play of bluish light in conjunction with the layered pattern of shade and shadow that gives this composition its strong visual impact.

9.28 A supplementary frisket allows the farther, lower cubic form to be airbrushed in two steps.

9.29 The fourth and final full frisket allows for the introduction of shadows cast on the freestanding gridwork.

As you continue to use the airbrush you will begin to consider it as a means of seeing the world around you in a different way. You will become more aware of the behavior of light, seeing both the structure of the "big picture" as well as the fine details of the "small picture." As designer Achille Castiglioni famously stated: "To innovate, you must first learn how to look." This more voracious way of seeing will enable you to bathe your illustrated architectural designs in the same clear light that they receive in reality.

10 Gallery: George Dombek

George Dombek's airbrush watercolor paintings of architectural subjects are only a fraction of his wide-ranging subject matter, but they are instructive in their focus on the play of bright sunlight on architectural form and detail. His central concern is the critical act of seeing and recording geometries in the visual field: patterns of shade and shadow falling across spatially displaced planes, negative and positive spaces of light and dark, and similarly formal qualities of the visual experience. Regardless of the subject matter, each illustration embodies the forceful interplay of silhouette and the complex overlapping perspective of grid patterns. This is particularly evident in his renderings of the visual "carpentry" of run-down tobacco barns. In each case, cropping of the image is essential to the scheme of spatial illusion—whether it is a close-up, depth-defying grid of timbers or a tilted perspective of overhead roof beams.

Dombek's work shows a fascination for the color intensity characteristic of the watercolor medium. This is apparent in everything from his early illustrations of sunlit fruit crates in rural Arkansas to his later illustrations of the behavior of sunlight on slatted and gridded architectural forms. A selection of images are showcased on the following pages. All illustrations are watercolor on watercolor paper. Further examples of George Dombek's work can be found at www.georgedombek.com.

Top:
10.1 *Blue Grid*, 30 x 42 in (76 x 107 cm)

Bottom:
10.2 *Crosses*, 30 x 42 in (76 x 107 cm)

10.3 *Light-play*, 24 x 60 in (61 x 152 cm)

10.4 *Architecture Number 6*, 38 x 42 in (97 x 107 cm)

10.5 *San Francisco Windows*, 38 x 58 in (97 x 147 cm)

10.6 *Tree Grid*, 30 x 30 in (76 x 76 cm)

10.7 *Tour de Tree*, 40 x 60 in (102 x 152 cm)

10.8 *White Sunday*, 16 x 20 in (41 x 51 cm)

10.9 *Wooden Rhythm*, 40 x 60 in (102 x 152 cm)

10.10 *Republic Steel*, 30 x 42 in (76 x 107 cm)

10.11 *New Center Street Bridge*, 24 x 60 in (61 x 152 cm)

10.12 *Barn on a Plain*, 30 x 42 in (76 x 107 cm)

Glossary

acetate. Transparent plastic produced in sheets and rolls, used in airbrushing as a stencil material.

acrylic flow release. Additive used to increase the viscosity of acrylic airbrush paint.

acrylic paint. A synthetic, plastic emulsion paint that, being soluble in water, allows very thin, transparent washes to be applied, as in the classical watercolor technique.

cfm. Cubic feet per minute; units used to measure the volume of air.

chroma. The intensity of brightness of a color. Sometimes referred to as "saturation" or "chromaticity."

cold-press. Surface designation of medium-type boards and papers produced under pressure from cold rollers.

color cup. Airbrush-mounted reservoir for feeding liquid medium into the airbrush.

compressed air. Air under pressure.

compressor. An appliance for producing and storing compressed air.

cut. The area removed from a frisket or stencil.

depth cues. The visual signals used to increase the illusion of depth in two-dimensional images.

dual-action. Type of airbrush in which depression of the trigger delivers air and retraction of the trigger delivers liquid medium to the airflow.

extender. Additive used to increase the transparency of acrylic airbrush medium.

external-mix. Type of airbrush in which the liquid medium is atomized outside the airbrush head.

fade. To gradually reduce tonal or color strength.

fan. The width of a spray produced by the airbrush.

freehand. Airbrushing without the aid of a mask.

frisket. A general term to describe different types of mask used to protect areas from airbrush spray.

frisket film. Transparent, adhesive-backed mask that is cut while in position on the artwork.

frisket knife. Thin-bladed scalpel, such as an X-Acto knife, with an extremely angled tip incorporating a fixed blade.

gradation. A gradual, smooth change of airbrushed value or chroma.

gravity-feed. Type of airbrush that uses gravity to transfer the liquid medium into the airbrush from a reservoir mounted above the handset.

hand-held mask. Nonadhesive mask manually positioned on the artwork surface.

hard edge. A sharp, crisp edge created by airbrushing over friskets, stencils, and masks.

highlight. A bright point of light, reflected light, or "starburst."

hot-press. Surface designation of smooth board or paper produced under pressure from hot rollers.

hue. A color on the color wheel (e.g., red, orange, yellow, green, blue, violet).

ink. Shellac-based liquid color medium.

internal-mix. Type of airbrush in which the liquid medium is atomized inside the body of the airbrush.

light source. The point or direction from which light emanates.

liquid frisket. A removable liquid masking agent, such as rubber cement.

mask. A protective covering used to block or filter areas of the artwork not to be painted.

medium. A binder or vehicle into which pigments are mixed. In a more general sense, medium also describes the various types of pigment used in image-making, such as ink, watercolor, and acrylic.

mismatched lines. White lines or halos that appear along the edges of airbrushed shapes when secondary friskets are imperfectly cut or when replaced friskets are misaligned.

modulate. To regulate or vary the value of a tone or color.

moisture trap. A filter for removing water from compressed air.

monochromatic. Of or having one hue.

opaque medium. Nontransparent paint, such as gouache or acrylic.

overlay. A transparent sheet laid over artwork as a ground to be worked on.

overspray. The atomized material that escapes the directed spray, or the application of secondary spraytones to alter the color or effect.

paint. A mixture of medium and pigment.

perspective. The creation of the illusion of depth using converging lines.

picture plane. The imaginary plane represented by the physical surface of the artwork.

pigment. A material used as a colorant in paint.

psi. Pounds per square inch. A unit used to measure air pressure.

reflected light. Light that hits adjacent surfaces after striking an object.

regulator. The device that controls the air pressure for compressed air.

render. To depict in drawing or painting; usually referring to the application of color or halftones.

resist. A substance applied to the artwork to prevent the medium from reaching the support surface.

respirator. Face mask designed to filter contaminants from the air.

retouching. The alteration of a photograph or an airbrushed image.

rough (R). Surface designation of robust, textured watercolor paper or board.

score. To indent the surface of board or paper.

shade. The unlit areas on the surface of an illuminated object.

shadow. A dark figure projected onto another surface by an object intercepting rays of light.

single-action. Type of airbrush in which depressing the trigger delivers air and liquid medium simultaneously.

soft edge. A diffused edge created with an airbrush, usually without a mask or with a hand-held or loose mask positioned slightly above the surface of the artwork.

spraytone. Deposit of tone or color resulting from a fine mist of air and atomized medium.

stencil. A thin sheet from which shapes or patterns are cut, through which liquid medium is sprayed to the surface below.

spatter. The coarse-textured effect caused by the controlled spraying of dots.

stipple. The technique or process of drawing or painting with dots instead of lines.

supplementary frisket. A secondary, auxiliary, or localized frisket used to airbrush a complex detail.

support. The material or surface on which the paint is applied.

tack. Degree of adhesiveness.

template. A manufactured or custom-made guide used to develop a shape.

thinner. A dilution agent, such as lacquer thinner.

tone. The tint or shade of a color.

tooth. The surface texture of paper or board.

transparent medium. A paint, ink, or dye that permits the paper surface, undercoat, or lines to show through.

two-dimensional plane. The flat surface represented by the artwork support.

value. Degree of lightness or darkness.

viscosity. The degree of fluidity of paint.

watercolor. Pigment ground up with water-soluble gums that, when moistened with plain water, provide a transparent stain applied in thin washes to white paper.

Appendix A
Gallery of Student Illustrations: Techniques

Following are brief descriptions of the processes used to create the images in chapter 1.

Figure 1.1
FAÇADE
8 x 12 in (20 x 30 cm)
This small, three-color illustration simply extends the basic principles explained in the cube exercise in chapter 5. The subtly textured appearance of sunlit façades results from a light spatter effect.

Figure 1.2
VILLA SAVOYE, POISSY
This illustration of Le Corbusier's seminal house design also involved three colors, in addition to black, and three friskets. To enliven the image, two different blacks were used: mars black and lampblack. The modular joints in the foreground plane were delineated with a technical pen.

Figures 1.3 and 1.4
ARCHITECTURAL DETAILS
Both of these building details resulted from student photographic assignments that explored the patterns of shade and shadow caused by the play of light on repetitive forms (fig. 1.3) and dissimilar planes (fig. 1.4).

Figure 1.5
INDUSTRIAL PLANT
This illustration comprises airbrush- and paintbrush-applied watercolor washes. Some unintentional scarring, caused during the frisket-cutting stage, made the color darken in those areas. This created an unexpected patina—an effect entirely in keeping with the spirit of the image.

Figure 1.6
ENTRANCE
During the airbrushing of the sky portion of this illustration, a paint spillage ruined this area. However, the image was saved by trace-cutting along the skyline and gluing the rescued architectural portion to a sheet of blue pastel paper.

Figure 1.7
THE EXPERIENCE MUSIC PROJECT, SEATTLE
18 x 23 (46 x 58 cm)
Using acrylic paint and employing the basic starter palette described on page 29, the student employed extensive color mixing, experimenting with color effects on scraps of paper before introducing them into the artwork. In order to simulate the curving dynamic of Frank O. Gehry's building, the student also experimented with freehand airbrushing and hand-held masks for some of its isolated, soft-edged shapes.

Figure 1.8
ATRIUM, MIAMI
This illustration, together with figure 1.9 and those figures on the facing page, demonstrate the need of some beginning students to challenge themselves with highly complicated renderings. Although compelling images do not always result from complexity of content, they can be made in airbrush—their achievement often demanding extensive frisket-cutting.

Figure 1.9
GRID PORTAL
The composition of this illustration just avoids a dead-center symmetry to achieve a view of middleground planes seen through the delineation of the foreground gridwork. Its potential flatness is also avoided by the play of light, the addition of color, and, of course, the dynamic of the perspective drawing.

Figure 1.10
CORNICE
This four-color illustration reduced the need for a new, full frisket between color changes by working on locally-frisketed portions while the remainder of the format was protected by an ancillary paper mask.

Figure 1.11
FRIEZE DETAIL
The intricacy of this illustration embodies a combination of airbrush and technical penwork. After the airbrush established the main shadow and the horizontal bands of shade, the technical pen

was used to introduce the detail seen on the figure, much of it applied in dot formation to remain in keeping with the airbrush.

Figure 1.12
MATERIALS MONTAGE
This unusual choice for an inaugural color airbrush illustration was made by a student who wanted a vehicle with which to practice the rendition of different building materials. Notice the two grills at the bottom of the central building; these were created by spraying through a found mask of perforated paper, a technique discussed in chapter 4.

Figure 1.13
KAHN RESIDENCE, PACIFIC PALISADES, CALIFORNIA
12 x 12 in (30 x 30 cm)
This small perspective of a private house designed by the Central Office of Architecture was created using the photocopy frisket technique. The main challenge was the blockwork façade, which necessitated a painstaking, two-stage frisket cutting sequence—a procedure hampered by an obliterating overspray.

Figure 1.14
SMITH HOUSE, DARIEN, CONNECTICUT
Here, again, the airbrush was used to depict light—this time the nighttime glow of electric illumination. This illustration of Richard Meier's classic house design is unusual in the filigree effect of the lighter portion of the sky seen through the foliage of background trees. This effect was achieved by applying a rubber cement mask with a sponge prior to the final spraying stage. The heavy black of the landscape trees was introduced before the rubber cement was rubbed away.

Figure 1.15
KIMBELL ART MUSEUM, FORT WORTH, TEXAS
The subject matter depicted in this image of Louis Kahn's museum provided an excellent airbrush vehicle for the student to simulate reflected light seen in the foreground planes. It also allowed the student to experiment with the sponge-applied foliage effect seen on the skyline trees and explained in chapter 8.

Figure 1.16
LIGHT TRANSITIONS
This dramatically illuminated architecture is airbrushed from a photograph of an unidentified building. It was specifically selected by the student in order to practice the airbrushing of cylindrical planes. The foreground presents the technique for adding grass effects, demonstrated in chapter 7. The effect is created by adding a series of flicking lines drawn with a white Prismacolor pencil at the end of the spraying stage.

Figure 1.17
STUDY MODEL
While producing the preliminary underdrawing for this illustration of a Frank O. Gehry study model, the student made many modifications that involved much erasing, which slightly abraded the surface of the paper. This resulted in a "happy accident" while airbrushing, creating the beautiful texture seen on the rear wall.

Figure 1.18
INTERIOR
Using a single frisket, this illustration was produced very quickly. Its effortless portrayal of the pattern of light, shade, and shadow is the kind of rendition that the airbrush can do so effectively.

Figure 1.19
ELEVATION DETAIL
This is another illustration that was rescued following a paint spillage—this time on the building elevation. Undaunted, the student trace-cut and unceremoniously removed the damaged portion and, after plugging it jigsaw-fashion with a new piece of board, continued airbrushing.

Figure 1.20
SCIENCE MUSEUM AT THE CITY OF ARTS AND SCIENCES, VALENCIA
Worked on a 24 x 22 in (61 x 56 cm) format, on a 30 x 40 in (70 x 76 cm) illustration board, and bravely using Santiago Calatrava's rhythmical building elevation as a source, this illustration involved four applications of frisket film. Although suffering from excessive buildup of overspray—especially in the darker regions and in the sky area—and the clutter of discarded frisket around its ill-defined border, the illustration reflects a spirited and exuberant first attempt at a large-scale work.

Appendix B: Matting

B.1 22 x 30 in (56 x 76 cm) illustration in a 32 x 40 in (81 x 102 cm) mat

B.2 8 x 12 in (20 x 30 cm) illustration in a 16 x 20 in (41 x 51 cm) mat

Sometimes illustrations must be matted for presentation. The mat is an important part of the viewing of the artwork because it functions as a "window" through which the illustration is seen. Consequently, the mat should not dominate or interfere with the illustration's ability to engage the viewer's eye. Some basic guidelines for matting an architectural illustration follow.

ILLUSTRATION-MAT RELATIONSHIP

Although the figure-ground relationship between the illustration and its mat is a question of personal preference, the following basic compositional tips may be helpful.

Mat size. Generally speaking, the larger the illustration, the less the need for a large border. For example, illustrations around 22 x 30 in (56 x 76 cm) in size work well in 32 x 40 in (81 x 102 cm) mats (fig. B.1). Smaller illustrations can take relatively larger surrounds—illustrations up to 8 x 12 in (20 x 30 cm) work well in 16 x 20 in (41 x 51 cm) mats (fig. B.2). Illustrations around 16 x 20 in (41 x 51 cm) are comfortable in 24 x 28 in (61 x 71 cm) mats. Generally, the border surrounding an illustration of any size should not be less than 4 to 4½ in (10 to 11 cm) in width. Borders smaller than this appear pinched.

Positioning the illustration in the mat. There are two strategies for positioning the illustration in the mat. The first option is to center the illustration on the mat, allowing for equal borders at the top, bottom, and each side (fig. B.3, left). The second option is to place the image slightly higher than halfway up the mat, allowing the bottom border to be wider than the top and sides (fig. B.3, right). This strategy is based on the eye's tendency to search for some resistance to the pull of gravity. In other words, the eye may perceive an image placed in the dead center of the mat as sliding down. Making the bottom border wider counteracts this optical illusion by giving the image a visual "ledge" or "cushion" on which to rest.

Mat color. Richly colored backgrounds can interfere with the colors in the image and detract from the information that it conveys. Therefore, as a general rule, neutral mats, such as white, gray, or black, should be favored. When in doubt, white is a good choice because its unsullied neutrality encourages the viewer to focus exclusively on the artwork, whether the illustration is in color or in black and white.

Matting can be avoided completely if the airbrushed image is positioned centrally on the support, with equal borders at the top and sides and a slightly wider border at the bottom (fig. B.4). If the borders are well protected during airbrushing and the edge of the image is carefully maintained during frisket changes, there is no need to mat the completed illustration. However, if the illustration's edge is imperfect—if paint has crept under the surrounding mask—the best way to conceal it is to display the artwork behind a mat window cut slightly smaller than the size of the illustration (fig. B.5).

When the edge of an illustration is perfect but the border of the support is too narrow, you can use a matting method that provides a "double frame" appearance (fig. B.6). Here the mat window is larger than the image, usually allowing a ½ in (1 cm) border on all sides of the illustration. Thus, the edge of the illustration remains visible inside the mat window.

The same method applies to illustrations airbrushed on watercolor paper. As previously mentioned, before painting, the edge of watercolor paper is traditionally torn to size and the image is usually painted all the way to the edges. The traditional matting method leaves this edge exposed, with a ½ in (1 cm) border between it and the window (fig. B.7). To achieve this, first attach the illustration to a smaller backing board, such as foamcore. (The backing board should be about 2 in (5 cm) bigger on all sides than the illustration.) Affix the watercolor illustration to the backing board using a strip of double-sided acid-free tape along the top edge. Then

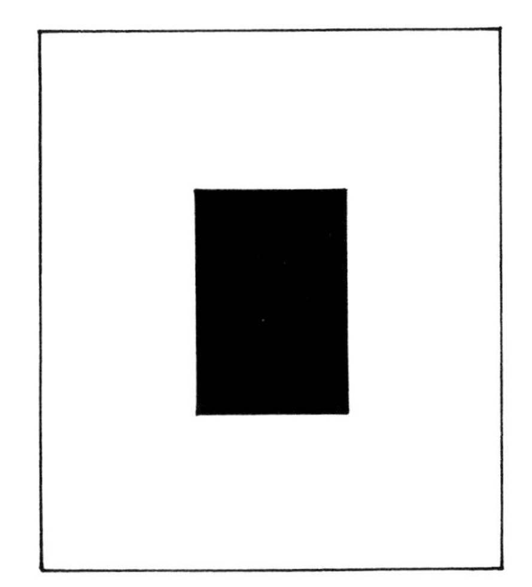

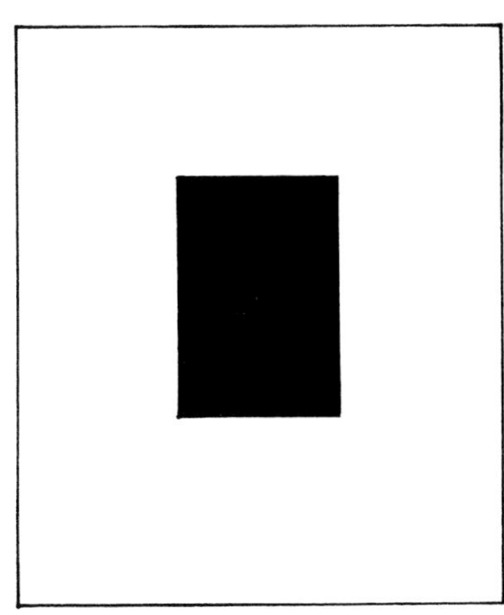

B.3 Two positioning strategies: Dead center (left) and above center (right)

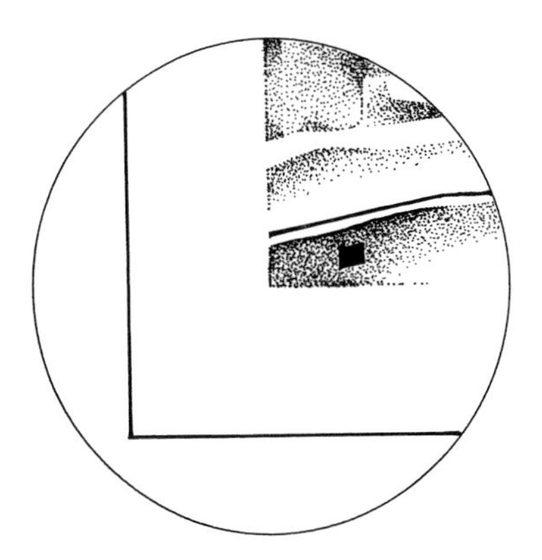

B.4 Airbrushed image shown unmatted on the support

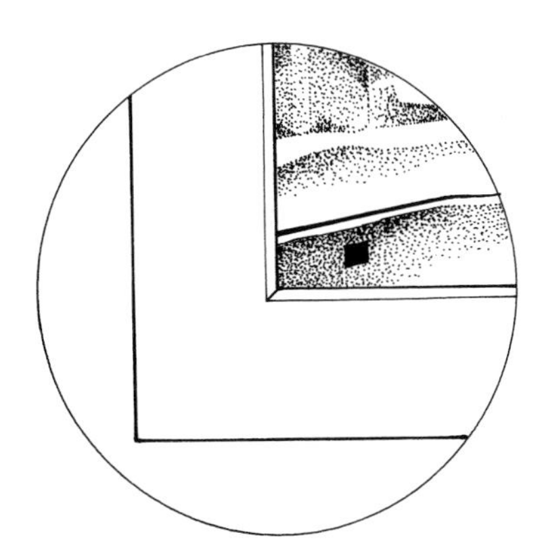

B.5 Mat window cut slightly smaller than the size of the illustration

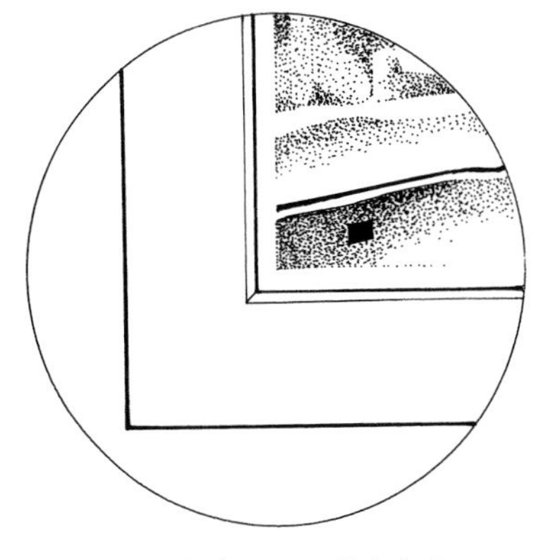

B.6 Mat window cut slightly larger than the size of the illustration

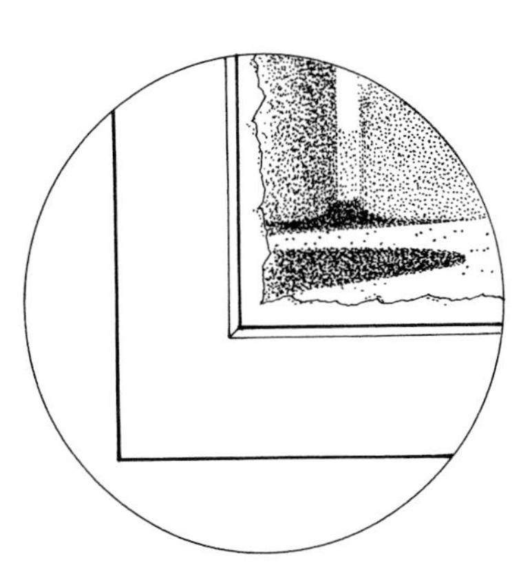

B.7 Floated watercolor paper illustration

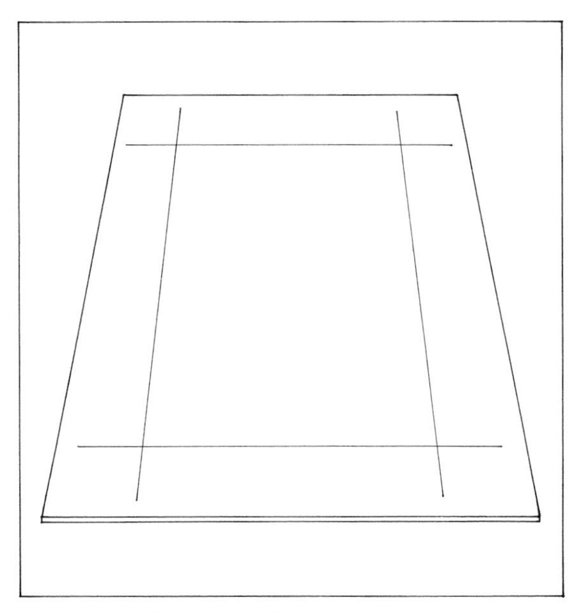

B.8 Drawing the outline of the area to be cut on the back of the mat board

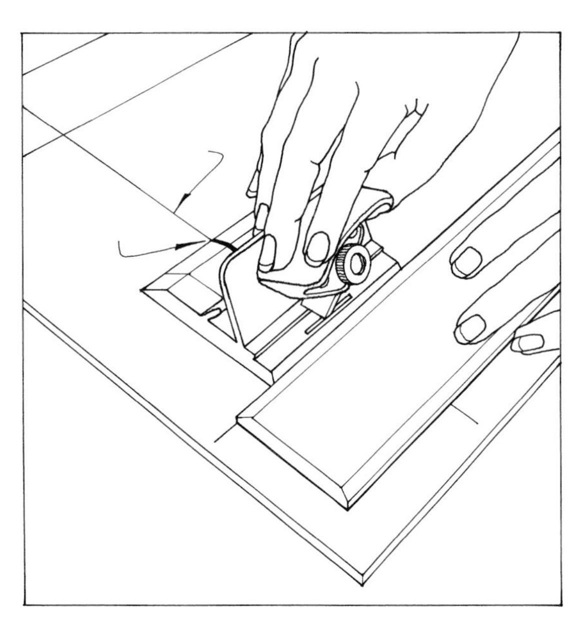

B.9 Positioning the mat cutter

place a mat board, with a window cut to allow a ½ in (1 cm) border around the artwork, over the illustration. This method causes the illustration to appear to "float" inside the window.

CUTTING A BEVELED WINDOW MAT

To cut a beveled window into a mat board using a custom mat cutter, first use a straightedge to measure and draw the outline of the area to be cut on the back of the mat board (fig. B.8). To facilitate the precise marking of the window, some mat cutters (for example, the Logan 400) incorporate an extendable, built-in measurement bar.

Place the mat face down on a base of corrugated board or cardboard. Then, using a metal straightedge precisely aligned to one side of the marked window as a guide, position the mat cutter so that its guide mark coincides with the line intersecting the line of the cut (fig. B.9). Apply downward pressure so that the angled blade fully penetrates the mat board. Holding the straightedge secure with one hand, pull the cutter toward you until the cutter guidemark coincides with the intersecting line at the other end of the cut.

Tilt back the blade and remove the mat cutter from the mat board. Rotate the mat cutter counterclockwise and repeat this operation for the remaining three sides of the window.

Appendix C:
Iwata Eclipse HP-CS: Tips and Troubleshooting

Before starting each session, retract, rotate, and reseat the fluid needle (17) in a new position. This ensures even wear on the nozzle and the needle, and thus extends their working lives.

The cut-away handle (19) is a special feature on the Eclipse airbrush. Its purpose is to allow dried paint that may have formed at the tip of the airbrush to be cleaned away without removing the needle or handle. To do this, simply grip the exposed needle chucking nut (18) between your thumb and forefinger. Pull back on the needle chucking nut while

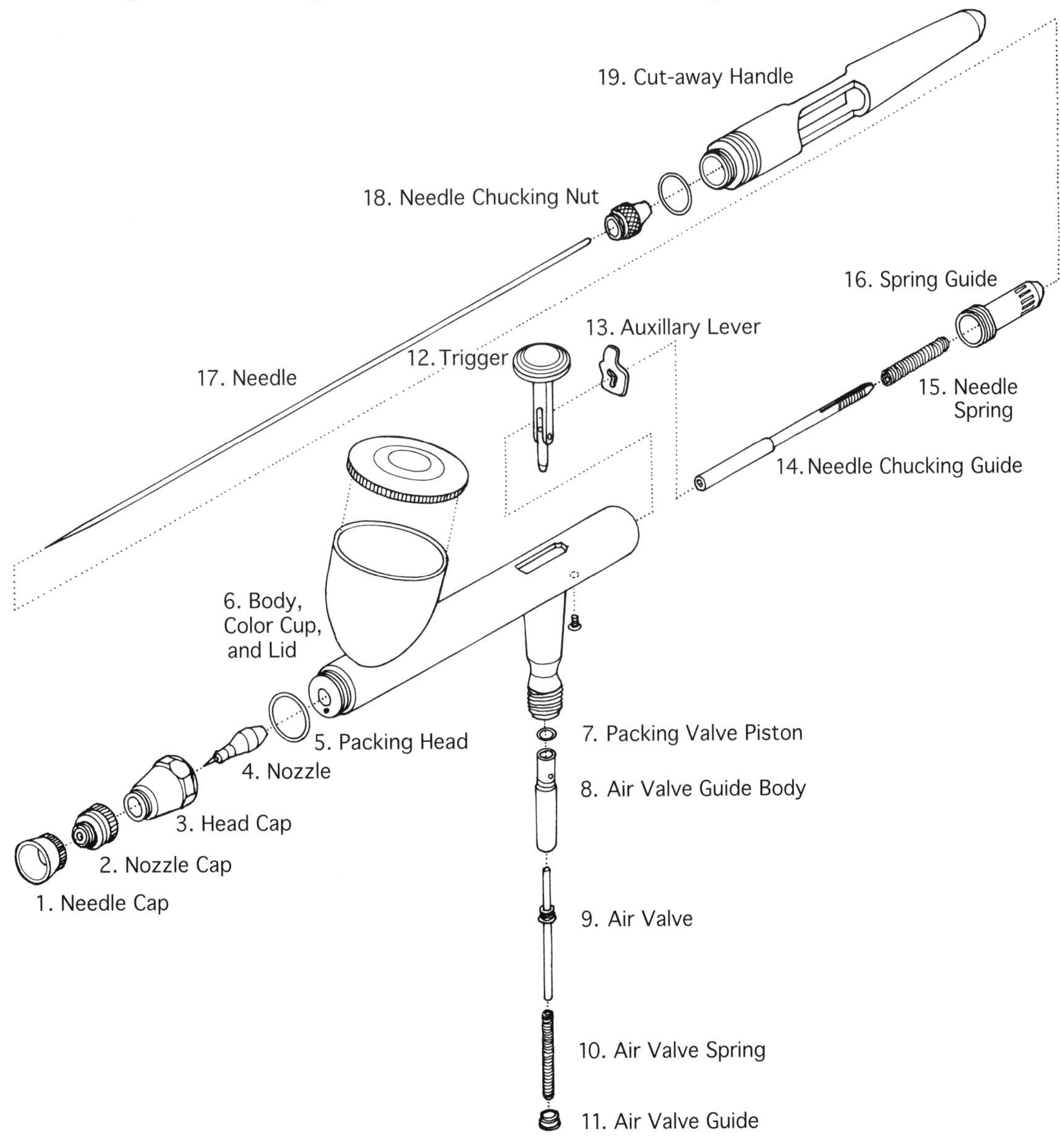

simultaneously depressing the trigger (12). This will allow large amounts of paint to flow past the needle and tip, thus freeing up any dried clogs of paint. Repeat this procedure several times until the airbrush is free of obstructions and sprays normally.

It is also worth mentioning the most common airbrush problem: when the airbrush fails to spray. Either you have forgotten to switch on the compressor power supply or the handset is clogged and requires cleaning. When the airbrush spray pattern appears erratic, causing spitting, it is usually because the needle isn't clean or because there is an air leak in the hose. Check the hose for leakage, tighten its connections, and, if necessary, rebind each connector with white plumber's tape to ensure an airtight seal. Also, remove the needle for a thorough cleaning, so no traces of pigment remain.

Always remove the needle before replacing the nozzle. Once the nozzle is in place and secure, then replace the needle. This will prevent damage to the nozzle when tightening the nozzle head cap (3).

An irregular spray pattern can also be caused by a buildup of moisture in the air supply. However, this should not happen if your hose is fitted with a moisture trap or if the compressor regulator has a moisture trap.

If the airbrush continues to malfunction after you have taken the previous precautions, you could try blowing some flow release or solvent, such as Medea Airbrush Cleaner, through the airbrush into a mist control box. As a last resort, take the airbrush completely apart and soak the parts overnight in a solvent. A recommended solvent is EZ-Air Airbrush Cleaner made by Golden Artist Colors, Inc. After cleaning each component with paper tissue, including the control lever spring, reassemble the airbrush. (Note: Do not use pliers to assemble or disassemble the airbrush. The parts are designed to be hand-tightened only.)

Appendix D: Manufacturers and Suppliers

United States

Arches Papers
Canson Inc.
21 Industrial Drive
South Hadley, MA 01075
Tel: 800-628-9283
Fax: 413-533-6554
E-mail: arches@canson-us.com
www.canson-us.com

Badger Airbrush Co.
9128 West Belmont Avenue
Franklin Park, IL 60131
Tel: 847-678-3104
Fax: 847-671-4352
www.badger-airbrush.com

Bear Air
15 Tech Circle
Natick, MA 01760
Tel: 800-BEARAIR
E-mail: bearbrush@aol.com
www.bearair.com

Crescent Cardboard Company L.L.C.
100 West Willow Road
Wheeling, IL 60090
Tel: 847-537-3400
Fax: 847-537-7153
E-mail: kmccarthy@crescentcardboard.com
www.crescentcardboard.com

Golden Artist Colors, Inc.
Bell Road
New Berlin, NY 13411
Tel: 607-847-6154
Fax: 607-847-6767
www.goldenpaints.com

Grafix
Graphic Art Systems, Inc
19499 Miles Road
Cleveland, OH 44128
Tel: 216-581-9050
Fax: 216-581-9041
E-mail: info@grafixarts.com
www.grafixarts.com

M. Graham & Co.
PO Box 215
West Linn, Oregon 97068-0215
Tel: 503-656-6761
E-mail: colormaker@mgraham.com
www.mgraham.com

HK Holbein
175 Commerce Street
PO Box 555
Williston, VT 05495
Tel: 800-682-6686
Fax: 802-658-5889
E-mail: holbeinhk@aol.com
www.holbeinhk.com

Iwata-Medea, Inc.
PO Box 14397
Portland, OR 97293
Tel: 503-253-7308
Fax: 503-253-0721
E-mail: info@iwata-airbrush.com
www.iwata-airbrush.com

NOTE: Iwata-Medea, Inc. are also the U.S. distributors of Frisk products.

Paasche Airbrush Company
7440 West Lawrence Avenue
Harwood Heights, IL 60706
Tel: 708-867-9191
Fax: 708-867-9198
E-mail: paascheair@aol.com
www.paascheairbrush.com

Winsor & Newton
ColArt Fine Arts & Graphics Ltd.
11 Constitution Avenue
Piscataway, NJ 08855
www.winsornewton.com

United Kingdom

Arches watercolor paper
John Purcell Paper
15 Rumsey Road
London SW9 0TR
Tel: 020 7737 5199
Fax: 020 7737 6765
E-mail: www.johnpurcell.net

Arches watercolor paper
Tollit and Harvey
Olmedow Road
King's Lynn
Norfolk PE30 4LW
Tel: 01553 696600
Fax: 01553 767235
www.tollitandharvey.co.uk

Badger Airbrush products
Shesto Ltd.
Unit 2, Sapcote Trading Centre
374 High Road
Willesden
London NW10 2DH
Tel: 0208 451 6188
E-mail: richard@shesto.co.uk
www.shesto.co.uk

Frisk Film products and
X-acto knives
Bell Creative Supplies Ltd
Unit C5 Wardley Point
Fallons Road
Wardley Industrial Estate
Worsley
Greater Manchester M28 2NY
Tel: 0161 727 8388
Fax: 0161 794 5705
www.bellcreative.co.uk

Golden Artists Colors
Global Art Supplies Ltd.
Unit 8
Leeds Place
Tollington Park
London N4 3QW
Tel: 0207 281 2451
Fax: 0207 281 7693

HK Holbein products
Jackson's Art Supplies
PO Box 29568
London N1 4WT
Tel: 0870 241 1849
Fax: 020 7354 3641
E-mail: Sales@Jacksonsart.com
www.Jacksonsart.com

M. Graham & Co.
T. N. Lawrence & Son Ltd.
208 Portland Road
Hove BN3 5QT
Tel: 0845 644 3232
E-mail: artbox@lawrence.co.uk
www.lawrence.co.uk

Iwata airbrush, ComArt paint
and Paasche airbrush products
Rick J. Smith
The Airbrush Company Ltd
39 Littlehampton Road
Worthing
West Sussex BN13 1QJ
Tel: 01903 266991
Fax: 01903 830045
E-mail: airbrush@lineone.net

Winsor & Newton
Whitefriars Avenue
Harrow
Middlesex HA3 5RH
Tel: 020 8427 4343
Fax: 020 8863 7177
E-mail: s.miller@colart.co.uk
www.winsornewton.com

Index